DK EYEWITNESS TRAVEL

TOP 10
STOCKHOLM

PAUL EADE

Top 10 Stockholm Highlights

The Top 10 of Everything

CONTENTS

Stockholm Area by Area

Streetsmart

Within each Top 10 list in this book, no hierarchy of quality or popularity is implied. All 10 are, in the editor's opinion, of roughly equal merit.

Front cover and spine Stortorget, Gamla Stan
Back cover Panoramic view of Stockholm
Title page Colourful buildings on Stortorget, Gamla Stan

The information in this DK Eyewitness Top 10 Travel Guide is checked regularly. Every effort has been made to ensure that this book is as up-to-date as possible at the time of going to press. Some details, however, such as telephone numbers, opening hours, prices, gallery hanging arrangements and travel information are liable to change. The publishers cannot accept responsibility for any consequences arising from the use of this book, nor for any material on third-party websites, and cannot guarantee that any website address in this book will be a suitable source of travel information. We value the views and suggestions of our readers very highly. Please write to: Publisher, DK Eyewitness Travel Guides, Dorling Kindersley, 80 Strand, London WC2R 0RL, Great Britain, or email travelguides@dk.com

Welcome to
Stockholm

Grand royal palaces and lush green parks. Densely packed Old Town streets and a sprawling archipelago. Swimming in peaceful Lake Mälaren by day and checking out the buzzing restaurant and bar scene in Södermalm by night. The Swedish capital is a city of amazing contrasts, and with Eyewitness Top 10 Stockholm, it's yours to explore.

The biggest city in Scandinavia, Stockholm is your gateway to a world of clean and compact living, sleek design and rustic cuisine. It is a place of short crisp winter days and long balmy summer nights. The city is made up of numerous islands, many with their own distinctive character, from colourful and historic **Gamla Stan** to leafy **Djurgården** and elegant **Östermalm**.

Witness an ill-fated symbol of Sweden's period as European power player during the 17th century at the incredible **Vasamuseet**, before delving deeper into the country's history at **Nordiska Museet** and **Historiska Museet**. Behold the pomp and splendour of the Swedish monarchy at **Drottningholm** and the **Royal Palace (Kungliga Slottet)**. Take in sweeping panoramic views from the tall tower of **Stadshuset**, get away from it all at **Hagaparken** or **Skansen**, or ride a seafront roller coaster at **Gröna Lund** theme park. Or simply share in the typically Swedish coffee-and-cake ritual *fika*, and watch the world go by through the window of a trendy café.

Whether you're coming for a weekend or a week, our Top 10 guide brings together the best of everything the city can offer, from hip **Södermalm** to sophisticated **Kungsholmen**. The guide gives you tips throughout, from seeking out what's free to the top archipelago activities, plus eight easy-to-follow itineraries, designed to help you visit a clutch of sights in a short space of time. Add inspiring photography and detailed maps, and you have the essential pocket-sized travel companion. **Enjoy the book, and enjoy Stockholm.**

Clockwise from top: **Nybroviken harbour; Gamla Stan; Stadsbiblioteket; Vaxholm Island, Stockholm Archipelago; Ericsson Globe; frozen Riddarfjärden; Brantingtorget, Gamla Stan**

Exploring Stockholm

With so many islands, activities and attractions to experience, it can be hard to know where to begin when it comes to discovering this surprising city. These two sightseeing itineraries will help you get the very best out of your visit to Stockholm.

The Nordiska Museet offers a comprehensive look at Swedish cultural history.

Two Days in Stockholm

Day ❶
MORNING
Start at the excellent **Vasamuseet** (see pp14–15) before taking a stroll through Galärparken to the **Nordiska Museet** (see pp30–31). Ulla Winbladh is nearby for a traditional Swedish lunch (see p81).
AFTERNOON
Take the tram along Strandvägen towards Strömkajen and take a ferry to the **Stockholm Archipelago** (see pp16–17). Pack a picnic and make the short trip to Fjäderholmarna, where you can swim from the rocks.

Day ❷
MORNING
Arrive early to admire panoramic views from **Stadshuset tower** (see pp22–3). Tour the **Royal Palace (Kungliga Slottet)** (see pp26–7) then wander the narrow streets of **Gamla Stan** with its many shops, cafes and restaurants (see pp84–91).
AFTERNOON
Take the ferry from Slussen across to **Djurgården** (see pp76–81), before

taking a stroll around **Skansen** (see pp12–13). Then make for **Gröna Lund** amusement park (see pp28–9), and end the day at the quirky ABBA-themed musical dining experience at *Mamma Mia! The Party* (note that booking is essential).

Four Days in Stockholm

Day ❶
MORNING
Hire City Bikes (citybikes.se, available April to October) and pedal around **Hagaparken** (see pp34–5). From there it is not far to Kungsholmen island, where **Petite France** is a decent place to have lunch (see p74).

The *Vasa* is the star of the Vasamuseet.

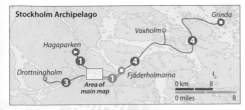

The island of Gamla Stan is the historic centre of Stockholm.

AFTERNOON
Cycle along the waterfront to the **Historiska Museet** *(see pp32–3)* and the **Nordiska Museet** *(see pp30–31)*. Then treat yourself to a high-end dinner at **Ekstedt** or **Gastrologik** *(see p81)*. Booking is essential.

Day ❷
MORNING
Start with breakfast at **Greasy Spoon** *(see p96)*, before taking in the fine views from Katarinavägen on your walk down to Slussen. From there hop on a short shuttle boat across to **Djurgården** and check out the fascinating **Vasamuseet** *(see pp14–15)*.
AFTERNOON
Explore **Skansen** *(see pp12–13)* or **Gröna Lund** *(see pp28–9, April to September)*. Hop back on the boat and return to Slussen, before experiencing the nightlife of hip Södermalm after dinner at **Nytorget Urban Deli** *(see p97)*.

Day ❸
MORNING
Start early at **Stadshuset** *(see pp22–3, May to September)*. Then take a boat at Stadshusbron for a cruise along Lake Mälaren to the Royal Palace, **Drottningholm** *(see pp24–5)*.
AFTERNOON
Visit the **Royal Palace (Kungliga Slottet)** *(see pp26–7)* and the Livrustkammaren armoury in the vaults beneath *(see pp58–9)*. Finally explore quaint **Gamla Stan** *(see pp84–91)*, before having dinner at **The Flying Elk** *(see p91)*.

Day ❹
MORNING
Begin the day at **Moderna Museet** *(see pp86–7)*. If it is the weekend, you can enjoy brunch at the café's buffet.
AFTERNOON
Set sail from nearby Strömkajen to the **Stockholm Archipelago** *(see pp16–17)*. Fjäderholmarna is 20 minutes away and perfect for picnics and swimming. If you wish to extend your journey, head to historic **Vaxholm** or pretty **Grinda** and stay another night.

Top 10 Stockholm Highlights

**Yachts moored among the islets
of the Stockholm Archipelago**

🔟 Stockholm Highlights

A city of contrasts dictated by the weather, Stockholm can offer Christmas-card scenes in winter and sun-drenched quaysides and waterways in summer. Unique museums and cool nightlife make it a year-round destination, but do wrap up in the winter.

1 Skansen
Part re-creation of Swedish traditional life, part zoo and part children's fair, this hilly park has something for everyone *(see pp12–13)*.

Vasamuseet 2
Get up close to the Vasa, which sank in Stockholm harbour on its maiden voyage in 1628 *(see pp14–15)*.

3 Stockholm Archipelago
An entire summer would not be enough to explore the archipelago's beaches, forests and seaside restaurants *(see pp16–17)*.

Stadshuset 4
The City Hall belies its stark exterior with magnificent halls, including the Prince's Gallery. The tower offers stunning views *(see pp22–3)*.

5 Drottningholm
Home to the royal family, this UNESCO World Heritage Site takes visitors back to 17th- and 18th-century grandeur. The extensive gardens are a delight *(see pp24–5)*.

6 The Royal Palace (Kungliga Slottet)
Built 57 years after its predecessor burned down in 1697, the Royal Palace is an extravagant combination of Italian, French and Swedish architectural influences *(see pp26–7)*.

7 Gröna Lund
Merging the best traditions of fairgrounds with thrill rides, Gröna Lund has something for everyone, from the 19th-century carousel to free-fall towers *(see pp28–9)*.

0 metres 500
0 yards 500

8 Nordiska Museet
Experience the Swedish way of life from the 16th to the 21st centuries in this museum, home to over 1.5 million exhibits – from jewellery to Strindberg's paintings *(see pp30–31)*.

9 Historiska Museet
Opened in 1943, this museum made its name with exhibits from the Viking era, as well as its collections from the early Middle Ages *(see pp32–3)*.

10 Hagaparken
A green oasis on the city's northern edge, this English-style park reveals its secrets along winding paths *(see pp34–5)*.

🔟⭐ Skansen

This open-air museum, which visualises Swedish history through the ages, was founded in 1891. It contains over 150 traditional buildings from around the country, dating from the 14th to the early 20th century – dismantled, transported and rebuilt on site. Nordic animals are kept in their natural habitats, surrounded by trees and plants from all over Sweden. Skansen changes naturally with the seasons: it's bustling and lively in summer, and calm and serene in winter.

1 Bredablick Tower

This 30-m (98-ft) high brick tower, was built by a royal physician who thought the views would be beneficial to people's wellbeing. It is no longer open to the public. Kids will enjoy the electric cars near the tower.

2 Funicular Railway

The mountain railway, Skansen's Bergbana, was built in 1897. Cable operated, it starts at the Hazelius entrance and is perfect for visitors with buggies or wheelchairs, or those simply wanting to enjoy a ride.

3 Historical Buildings

In the 19th-century town quarter, staff in traditional attire bake bread or make pottery. There are many farmsteads, churches and halls; several are open to public.

4 Lill-Skansen

A firm favourite since 1955 and rebuilt in 2012, the children's zoo has small animal enclosures, some of which children can enter.

5 Galejan Fairground

Enjoy the hand-painted carousels **(left)** and traditional sideshows.

7 Aquarium
Housed in the aquarium are 200 exotic marine species as well as the World of Monkeys, which features lemurs **(left)** and baboons.

8 Nordic Animals
The lynx, brown bear, wolf and moose enjoy roomy natural habitats on the park's northern cliffs, while Swedish sheep, goats and pigs live by the farmsteads.

9 Skansen Glassworks
Skilled glass-blowers use traditional tools to create designs unique to Skansen.

SPECIAL EVENTS

All of Sweden's major festivals are celebrated here – Midsummer, the traditional Christmas market, and New Year's Eve. Sing-a-long in Skansen is a Swedish institution featuring contemporary artists. It is held on Tuesday evenings in summer.

10 Gardens
These gardens **(below)** provide a contextual landscape to the buildings. The Skåne farmstead has a shady garden in keeping with rural southern Sweden, while the town quarters include allotments.

Främmestad Windmill, a historic building

Map of Skansen

6 Cafés and Restaurants
Have a romantic dinner at the Tre Byttor Tavern, savour a classic Swedish smörgåsbord at Solliden or grab a snack from a kiosk. Many visitors bring their own picnics.

NEED TO KNOW

MAP F4 ■ Djurgårdsslätten 49–51 ■ 08 442 80 00 ■ Tram 7; bus 44; ferry from Slussen to Djurgården ■ www.skansen.se

Open 10am onwards daily; check website for details about closing times during the year.

Adm 120–180 kr (adults); 60 kr (6–15s); under 5s free. Aquarium: 120 kr (adults); 60 kr (6–15s); under 4s free. Prices depend on season and events.

■ Admission prices are at their highest in summer and during special events, and are significantly cheaper in winter.

■ Skansen Terrassen, open all year round, offers good-value meals, including a vegetarian option, an à la carte menu and children's dishes.

TOP 10 ⭐ Vasamuseet

An impressive warship built between 1626 and 1628, the *Vasa* had a fatal flaw – she was top heavy, with insufficient ballast. She capsized and sank shortly after setting sail on her maiden voyage. In 1961, her remarkably intact hull was raised after 333 years under water. She is now preserved under controlled conditions to prevent decay, along with a host of fascinating artifacts recovered during the salvage operation. The museum also tells the story of the *Vasa* and her recovery. Models and reconstructions bring it all to life, while getting up close to the vessel is a unique experience.

③ Upper Deck
Skilled carpenters restored the destroyed upper deck in the 1990s. While entire new parts were needed to complete it, original timber has been used as much as possible **(left)**.

④ Skeletons
The skeletons of around 15 sailors were found during the salvage operation. The exhibition Face to Face includes a fantasy "meeting" with some of the individuals from the *Vasa* in a film, and through a series of six facial reconstructions.

① Lion Figurehead
The many lion sculptures reflect the fact that King Gustav II Adolf, who commissioned the building of the vessel, was known as the Lion of the North. The crowning glory is the 3-m (10-ft) long lion figurehead at the bow.

② Objects
Several objects were recovered from the ship and sea bed. The upper gun deck alone yielded a chest of personal items – a felt hat, sewing tools, a comb, gloves, a keg, a wooden spoon, coins and some smaller belongings.

⑤ Gun Deck
The *Vasa* was a warship armed with powerful artillery; there were 48 24-pounder cast-iron guns on both its upper and lower gun decks **(above)**.

NEED TO KNOW

MAP Q4 ■ Galärvarvs-vägen 14 ■ 08 519 548 00 ■ Tram 7; bus 44 to Nordiska Museet/Vasamuseet and bus 69 to Djurgårdsbron; ferry from Slussen to Djurgården ■ www.vasamuseet.se/en

Open Jun–end-Aug: 8:30am–6pm daily; Sep–end-May: 10am–5pm daily (till 8pm Wed), closed 1 Jan and 23–25 Dec

Adm 130 kr (adults); 110 kr (students with valid student ID); under 19s free

■ The museum offers information sheets in 15 different languages, including English, German, Spanish and French. Guided tours are available in English – check website for times.

■ A restaurant serves both light refreshments and hot and cold food.

6 Stern

Many of the ship's 500 sculptures were centred on the stern **(above)**, a symbol of Sweden's might. Although it was badly damaged, it has been carefully restored to reveal the ornamentation.

Vasamuseet Floorplan

Key to Floorplan
- Ground floor
- Second floor
- Third floor
- Fourth floor

7 Sculptures

Several sculptures, including one of cherubs around the royal emblem, show how Gustav II Adolf wanted the world to see himself and Sweden.

8 Cannons

Most of the 64 cannons were salvaged in the 17th century, using a diving bell for the recovery operation.

The museum displays three of the largest, cast in bronze and weighing 1.2 tons each **(above)**.

9 Film

The rediscovery of the sunken *Vasa* by a maverick archaeologist and its painstaking raising from the seabed between 1959–61 is the subject of a short film shown in the museum.

10 The Vasa Museum Garden

The garden cultivates plants that would have been vital to the health of those aboard; rambling hops, harvested in late summer, would flavour and conserve beer.

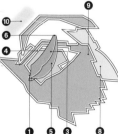

🔟 ⭐ Stockholm Archipelago

Stretching from Stockholm's outskirts to 60 km (37 miles) further east, the Stockholm Archipelago (Skärgård) is one of the most spectacular in the world. Consisting of around 30,000 islands and islets, it changes in character further east towards the open sea. Around 150 islands are inhabited; others are little more than bare rock. The archipelago comes alive in summer, when it is possible to take anything from a 25-minute boat hop to Fjäderholmarna to a two-hour-plus journey further afield.

1 Siaröfortet
Built as part of a defence line against naval forces, Siaröfortet is a warren of underground rooms, including barracks and a kitchen, plus guns embedded in the rock. It was decommissioned in the 1960s and has now been restored as a museum.

2 Sandhamn
The archipelago's yachting centre (below), Sandhamn's harbour is busy in summer – reflected in its lively party atmosphere. However, it also has a superb beach, Trouville, which is perfect for families.

3 Fjäderholmarna
An ideal day trip for those who want a taste of the archipelago without a long journey, this island (above) can be reached from May to October by frequent boats from Nybroplan or Slussen.

4 Norröra
The inspiration for Astrid Lindgren's TV series *Life on Seacrow Island*, Norröra has not changed a lot since 1964.

Map of Stockholm Archipelago

⑤ Finnhamn

A group of islands in the outer archipelago, Finnhamn is accessible by boat all year round, and its hostel welcomes guests from late spring till autumn. It also has an organic farm.

⑥ Ängsö Nationalpark

A national park since 1909, this is the place to experience a slice of old Sweden, much as it was hundreds of years ago. There is a signposted network of walking trails.

⑦ Grinda

One of the most popular archipelago destinations, Grinda offers a range of accommodation. The island's restaurants are highly popular in summer.

SOME MORE ISLANDS

Gällnö, a long-standing agricultural community, has striking landscapes of fields, meadows and glacial rocks. Själbottna, part of the Östra Lagnö nature reserve, is an excellent place to pitch a tent for the night and has secluded spots for bathing. Landsort, on the southernmost part of Öja, is home to the country's oldest functioning lighthouse. Rödlöga, which means "bathed in red", is a granite island on the archipelago's outer reaches, the last stop for regular boat services.

NEED TO KNOW

■ Ferry from Stockholm to the archipelago: Waxholmsbolaget
■ 08 614 64 50 ■ www. waxholmsbolaget.se

■ **Most of the islands listed on these pages are only accessible by scheduled boat services, so plan a trip carefully. Transport to many of the islands is very limited, sometimes to only one boat a day.**

■ **Catering facilities on the islands range from top-quality restaurants in the more popular destinations to simple cafés or kiosks, or in some remote instances, nothing at all. There are plenty of spots to enjoy a secluded picnic.**

⑧ Utö

In the southern part of the archipelago, Utö **(above)** offers outdoor activities such as canoeing and cycling. It has pretty beaches, good lodging options and cafés.

⑨ Arholma

The last outpost in the northern archipelago, Arholma has a beautiful landscape, most of which is a nature reserve. Sights here include a Midsummer pole in the form of a fully rigged mast and the Arholma watch beacon **(right)**, built in 1768 and now an art and crafts store.

⑩ Vaxholm

The archipelago's main town, Vaxholm is watched over by an old fortress and has many restaurants and cafés along the waterfront, where boats arrive. The island is also accessible by bus 670 from Stockholm.

Things to Do

1 Beaches and Swimming

The water might be quite chilly, but everyone goes swimming and paddling in the sea to cool off during the warmer summer months. The popular island of Grinda is about an hour away by ferry from central Stockholm, or you can simply take bus 428X from Slussen to Björkvik for swimming and sandy beaches with fine views across the water.

2 Farm Stays
www.ostanviksgard.se

Stay overnight at Östanviks Gård, a thriving archipelago farm, on the island of Nämdö, which dates back to the 16th century, or buy produce directly from its little shop.

3 Kayaking
www.ingmarsokajak.se

At Ingmarsö, visitors can rent single or double kayaks, or take a group tour around the nearby islands with a guide. The boat trip from Stockholm to Ingmarsö takes two and a half hours to the south jetty.

Children kayaking at Ingmarsö

Lunch at the Artipelag Museum

4 Day Trip with Lunch at an Archipelago Restaurant
www.visitskargarden.se

Numerous day trip packages take away the hassle of organizing travel and food, especially as tables in many restaurants can be fully booked in the high season. Visit the website for a choice of day trips.

5 Cottage Rentals
www.wimdu.com/stockholm-archipelago

Experience island life at close quarters by renting a cottage for a weekend or longer. Some islands have limited shopping facilities and often no alcohol store, so visitors may need to bring most or all their supplies with them. Destination Stockholms Skärgård has cottages to rent in the archipelago.

6 Boat Hiking
www.waxholmsbolaget.se/visitor/archipelago-traffic/island-hopping

The boat hiker's pass is valid for five days from the first journey and can be used on all Waxholmsbolaget boats. The pass comes with a map and suggested itineraries, including where to arrive at an island, hike across it and leave by ferry to continue on to another island.

⑦ Fishing

Going fishing with a hand tackle is allowed without a licence everywhere in the archipelago. For more serious fishing, hire a guide, many of whom offer boats, equipment, life vests and overalls. There are organized fishing trips from time to time – check at the tourist offices.

⑧ Winter Boat Trips
www.strömma.se

Enjoy the peace and tranquillity of the archipelago amidst snow and ice with a winter island-hopping cruise. Strömma offers a three-hour brunch cruise, departing at noon every Saturday and Sunday, aboard the 70-year-old *S/S Stockholm*.

Waxholmsbolaget steamboat

⑨ Steamboat Tours

Beautifully maintained veteran steamboats operate in high summer. Take one of the scheduled services for a day trip to Vaxholm or to one of the other islands such as Grinda. Or, choose a day or evening cruise with the option of lunch or dinner.

GETTING THERE AND AROUND

Boat timetables are available in printed form from all SL travel offices *(see p110)* and from tourist centres. Schedules can be complicated – some boats only sail on certain days – so check carefully; visitors taking a day trip must make sure they can get back. The fastest are the Cinderella ships, which cut journey times to the middle and outer archipelago. It is also possible to reach a lot of islands by bus, followed by a shorter boat trip – connections are given in the timetable. Winter boat schedules are limited. The main boat operator is Waxholmsbolaget *(see p107)* – its website, available in both Swedish and English, contains useful timetables and journey planners.

⑩ Camping

With the right of public access, anyone can pitch a tent in most open spaces. However, if you want fresh water and toilets, there are many designated camping spots, either free of charge, or for a small fee.

Camping in the archipelago

⭐ Stadshuset

The imposing red-brick City Hall is one of Stockholm's major landmarks, dominating the northern shore of Riddarfjärden bay. Completed in 1923, it is built in the National Romantic style, with the austere Nordic Gothic building juxtaposed with northern Italian features. Now containing government offices, the building can be viewed by guided tour only, but visitors can stroll at leisure through the courtyard and gardens, as well as climb the tower.

The Golden Hall ①

More than 18 million glass and gold mosaic fragments, the work of local artist Einar Forseth (1892–1988), adorn the impressive Golden Hall's walls **(right)**. They depict Swedish history using a Byzantine-inspired style.

② Statues

The beautiful gardens are filled with many statues. The steps to the water are flanked by two of Carl Eldh's sculptures: *The Song* and *The Dance*. On a 20-m (65-ft) pillar in the southeast corner is *Engelbrekt the Freedom Fighter* by Christian Eriksson.

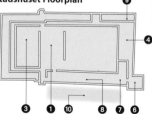

③ The Blue Hall

The venue for the Nobel Banquet, the Blue Hall was meant to have its bricks painted blue, but the architect Ragnar Östberg was so taken with the natural red that he had a last-minute change of heart.

Stadshuset Floorplan

④ Council Chamber

Stockholm's local councillors meet in this magnificent chamber, known as the Rådsalen in Swedish, **(left)** every third Monday. The 19-m (62-ft) high ceiling takes inspiration from the Swedish Viking Age. The public viewing gallery can accommodate about 200 spectators.

Previous pages The Royal Chapel nave at the Royal Palace (Kungliga Slottet)

6 Tower

Climb to the top of the 106-m (348-ft) tall tower **(left)** for superb views over the city from the open-air terrace. Visit the Tower Museum, located in the middle of the tower. A lift goes halfway to the top.

7 Oval Room

Weddings and civil partnerships are solemnized here. The walls are covered with a series of five 300-year-old tapestries woven in France.

NOBEL BANQUET

The Nobel Banquet is held in Stadshuset's Blue Hall annually on 10 December, after the Nobel Prize ceremony. Among the 1,300 guests are members of the Swedish Royal family and 250 students. There are lighthearted speeches by each of the Nobel Laureates, and ceremonial toasts. The banquet is also broadcast live on Swedish TV and radio.

8 Prince's Gallery

On the south side of Stadshuset are French windows offering a wonderful view of Lake Mälaren and Södermalm; the gallery's opposite wall **(above)** reflects this in a fresco called *Stockholm's Shores* (1922) painted by Prince Eugen, brother of King Gustav V.

9 Cellar Restaurant

Dine in Stadshuskällaren, the cellar restaurant *(see p75)*. It offers a wide range of classic Swedish dishes such as meatballs or marinated salmon.

5 Three Crowns

Sweden's heraldic symbol and national emblem of the three gold crowns – Tre Kronor – sits on top of the tower.

10 Gardens

The south-facing garden **(below)**, popular with sightseers and sunbathers, sits between Lake Mälaren and the Stadshuset building.

NEED TO KNOW

MAP K4 ■ Hantverkargatan 1 ■ 08 508 29 058 ■ open 8am–4:30pm Mon–Fri ■ www.stockholm.se/CityHall

Stadshuskällaren: www.stadshuskallarensthlm.se

■ To take the best photos of Stadshuset, walk eastwards to the path on the central railway bridge, Centralbron. From there, photographers can snap some great shots from across the water.

■ Adjacent to the hall, towards the street of Norr Mälarstrand, a kiosk sells ice creams and hot and cold drinks.

■ Groups of more than 10 require reservations.

Drottningholm

TOP 10 ⭐

The superbly preserved Drottningholm Palace and its grounds date from the 17th and 18th centuries, inspired by French models such as Versailles. On UNESCO's World Heritage list since 1991, the palace is the Swedish royal family's permanent home. Rooms in the southern wing are reserved for this purpose; the rest of the palace and grounds are open to the public. The grounds have trees dating from the palace's heyday as a royal court. It was abandoned, then fell into decay in the mid-19th century, but, after a six-year-long renovation from 1907, it began to be reused by the royal court.

① Queen Lovisa Ulrika's Library

Decorated in the 18th century by Jean Eric Rehn for the queen, the library includes paintings of historic events such as the crossing of the Great Belt in Denmark in 1658.

② The Nature Path

Close to the Chinese Pavilion, the nature path is a peaceful walk for anyone who wants to learn more about the flora and fauna and cultural history linked to the island of Lovön where Drottningholm is situated. The path is also signposted in Braille.

③ Court Theatre

This theatre, which is still preserved in its original condition, dates from 1766. Each summer it hosts around 30 performances, mainly 18th-century opera and ballet in period costume.

④ Queen Hedvig Eleonora's State Bedroom

Created over 15 years, the queen's ornate state bedroom **(below)** was the heart of the state reception suite in the 17th century.

5 Baroque Garden

The oldest part of the gardens **(below)** is laid out in a formal French style. Many of the statues were taken from cities captured by the Swedes, including the Wallenstein Palace in Prague.

7 Guards' Tent

Built in 1781 to serve as quarters for the dragoons of Gustav III, the Guards' Tent **(above)** resembles a tent in a Turkish army camp. The history of Drottningholm's Royal Guard is described in one of the rooms.

8 Staircase

Large statues of nine muses are placed on the balustrade, and *trompe-l'oeil* paintings by Johan Sylvius adorn the walls of the stair hall.

9 Studio of Evert Lundquist

The studio **(below)** is a museum housing oil paintings, drawings and engravings by Evert Lundquist (1904–94).

ROYAL RESIDENCE

Drottningholm Palace became the official royal residence in 1981, after falling in and out of favour with successive Swedish monarchs throughout its roughly 300-year lifetime up to that point. Often used as a summer residence during its first 150 years, it was abandoned throughout the reign of Charles XIV John (1818–44) and fell into decay, before being gradually repaired and restored under Oscar I, Oscar II and Gustav V.

10 Drottningholm by Boat

From May to October, steamships cruise on Lake Mälaren from the city centre to the palace. Boats depart from Stadshusbron, right beside the City Hall. Visit the palace's website for departures and fares.

6 Chinese Pavilion

At the time when this pavilion was built, as a surprise gift from King Adolf Fredrik to his wife Lovisa Ulrika in 1753, there was great interest in all things Chinese – the style is typically 18th-century Chinese.

NEED TO KNOW

- **MAP G2** ▪ 08 402 62 80
- www.kungahuset.se
- Ferry from Stockholm *(see pp106–7)*

Open 8 Jan–Mar: noon– 3:30pm Sat & Sun; Apr: 11am–3:30pm daily; May– Sep: 10am– 4:30pm daily; Oct: 11am– 3:30pm Fri– Sun; Nov–10 Dec: noon– 3:30pm Sat & Sun; 31 Dec–7 Jan: noon–3:30pm daily; closed 11–30 Dec

Adm 130 kr (adults); 65 kr (7–17s & students). Combination ticket inclu- des the Chinese Pavilion: 190 kr (adults), 90 kr (7–17s & students).

■ Drottningholm is a great day out for budget travellers – the gardens and Guards' Tent are all free and offer lots to see and do.

■ The visitor centre provides information and sells tickets. There is also a gift shop and restaurant.

TOP 10 ★ The Royal Palace (Kungliga Slottet)

Stunning rooms – more than 600 of them – and priceless jewels and artifacts are just some of the highlights of the Royal Palace. As one of the largest royal palaces still in use – it is the workplace of the monarchy – this is deservedly one of the city's showpiece attractions. Reminiscent of a Roman Baroque palazzo, it was designed by architect Nicodemus Tessin to replace the old Tre Kronor castle that burned down in 1697. Containing five different museums, the palace is guarded by the Royal Guard.

2 Bernadotte Apartments

The king receives foreign dignitaries in the East Octagonal Cabinet – the rooms are still furnished as they were in the mid-18th century. Do not miss the impressive library **(left)**.

3 Royal Chapel

The beautifully decorated chapel holds mass for employees of the Royal Court every Sunday; all staff can attend. It also holds classical music concerts.

1 Tre Kronor Museum

Built around the remains of a 12th-century defensive wall and housed in vaults from the 16th and 17th centuries, this museum takes visitors back to the original Tre Kronor palace, most of which was destroyed in a fire in 1697 **(below)**.

4 Gustav III's Museum of Antiquities

First opened in 1794, this museum includes a collection of statues bought by King Gustav III on a visit to Italy in 1783.

5 Hall of State

The highlight of the royal apartments, the Hall of State features the silver throne of Queen Kristina, who became queen-elect at the age of just five, later abdicating aged 28.

6 Guest Apartments

These beautiful rooms includes the Meleager Salon, a mix of Rococo and Gustavian styles. There is also a cabinet piano in mahogany with white-marble pilasters.

8 The Royal Guard

Drawn from the Swedish armed forces, the Royal Guard **(left)** has been protecting the palace since 1523. The Changing of the Guard takes place daily at midday, sometimes with music.

PALACE HISTORY

Kungliga Slottet was originally a 13th-century fortress, but evolved into a palace in the 17th century. Work to develop it began in 1692 under architect Nicodemus Tessin the Younger, but, in 1697, a fire destroyed most of the palace. Tessin submitted drawings for the new palace – the plan was for it to be built in about five years. However, the royal family was not able to move back in until 1754.

9 Karl XI's Gallery

This magnificent room is the palace's banqueting hall; official and state dinners, and a dinner in honour of Nobel Prize winners are all held here.

10 Treasury

The state regalia, including King Erik XIV's crown, are kept in deep cellar vaults. The 1676 silver font is still used at royal baptisms.

7 State Apartments

The royal family has lived at Drottningholm (see pp24–5) since 1981, but earlier inhabitants have left their mark here. The White Sea Ballroom **(above)** epitomizes the height of 18th-century elegance.

Royal Palace Floorplan

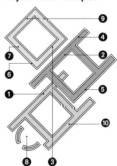

Key to Floorplan

Ground floor
First floor
Second floor

NEED TO KNOW

MAP M4 ■ Slottsbacken, Gamla Stan ■ 08 402 61 30 (weekdays 9am–noon) ■ Tunnelbana: Gamla Stan, Kungsträdgården; buses 2, 43, 55, 71, 76 ■ www.kungahuset.se

Open Oct–Apr: 10am–4pm Tue–Sun; May–Jun & Sep: 10am–5pm daily;

Jul–Aug: 9am–5pm daily

Royal Apartments: 150 kr (adults); 75 kr (7–18s & students); under 7s free ■ For details regarding visiting the different museums check the Kungahuset website.

■ The entry fee to the palace includes a 45-minute guided tour.

🔟 ⭐ Gröna Lund

Founded in 1883, Gröna Lund (the Green Grove), is Sweden's oldest amusement park – a mix of modern thrills and old-fashioned charm in an excellent waterside setting. Suitable for all ages, it offers a wide range of rides and attractions. Thrillseekers will love the park's seven roller coasters, but there are also more sedate rides – carousels with original 19th-century fittings and traditional sideshows. Gröna Lund is also a major concert venue, attracting big-name acts over the years, such as The Who, Bob Marley and Lady Gaga.

1 Roller Coasters

There are seven roller coasters at Gröna Lund, including the Jetline, which reaches speeds of 90 kmph (56 mph), and the wooden Twister by the waterfront. The Ladybird can be enjoyed by all ages.

2 Stages

There is both a large and small stage here, and some concerts are included in a day ticket, but it costs more for major events. A *Gröna Kortet*, or green card, provides unlimited admission, including to concerts, over a year.

Gröna Lund

3 The Old Carousel

The carousel **(left)** dates all the way back to 1892. Choose from riding lovable pigs, proud lions, traditional white horses or even a giraffe.

4 Free Fall Towers

One of the highest free fall towers in Europe at 80 m (262 ft), this ride is for intense thrill-seekers only, and definitely only those with no fear of heights. Take the Free Fall Tilt, which tilts before it falls, for an added thrill.

Gröna Lund rides

5 Mirror Pavilion

Pull silly faces and transform into absurd shapes in this temple of laughter (below).

6 Fun House

Lustiga Huset, or Fun House, is a genuine original from the 1920s with wacky rooms and wobbly bridges, and has been the inspiration and design for several fun houses in the world.

7 Restaurants and Bars

There are five restaurants and bars, plus kiosks selling traditional Swedish waffles and ice cream. Other outlets specialize in Thai and Mexican food, falafels, kebabs and burgers.

Eclipse 8

One of the latest additions to the park, this gravity-defying ride (right) takes exhilaration to new heights. At 122 m (400 ft) it is the highest StarFlyer in the world, and offers a 360-degree view of the capital.

9 Tunnel of Love

This tunnel takes you through a magical fairytale world decked with twinkling lights. Hold hands, steal a kiss or just enjoy its charm.

10 Flying Carpet

A wild and scary ride is what you would expect from a real flying carpet and this does not disappoint. Sit on the edge for a exciting ride.

HISTORY

In the early days, Gröna Lund's main attraction was a carousel moved by a horse. Founder Jacob Schultheis's son, Gustav Nilsson, laid the foundations of the modern attraction in the 1920s, adding rides and building the first concert stage. The park's popularity surged in the 1960s when it became Sweden's major music venue. But it remains true to its origins; most of the buildings date from the 19th century.

NEED TO KNOW

MAP R6 ▪ Lilla Allmänna gränd 9 ▪ 010 708 91 00 ▪ Tram 7; bus 44; ferry from Slussen to Djurgården ▪ www.gronalund.com

Open Apr–Sep, check website calendar for full details, as opening times vary according to the time of year

▪ Euros (notes only) are accepted at all the entrance and ticket booths, souvenir and photo shops, as well as kiosks and stands. The highest note accepted is €50, and change is given in kronor – the service centre exchanges euros for kronor.

▪ Step into the ABBA musical at *Mamma Mia! The Party* at Tyrol by Gröna Lund. Enjoy a three-course Mediterranean meal while musicians perform *Waterloo*, *SOS*, *Mamma Mia*, etc. Booking is essential.

TOP 10 ⭐ Nordiska Museet

A monument to Swedish cultural history, Nordiska Museet has exhibits that document everyday life in Sweden from the 16th century to the present. Created by Artur Hazelius, the founder of Skansen *(see pp12–13)*, Nordiska museet is housed in an imposing Renaissance-style building and the entrance features a huge statue of King Gustav Vasa. With over 1.5 million exhibits to see, visitors are spoilt for choice here – yet, much of the museum reflects simple everyday life in Sweden through the ages.

1 Traditions

When do Swedes eat *semlor*, cream buns with marzipan? Where did traditional Christmas celebrations originate? What are the origins of the Midsummer pole? The answers to these and other questions can be found in this exhibition, which covers festivals throughout the year.

2 Interiors

On display are re-created period homes and furnishings **(left)**, including parts of a drawing room from the 1880s and a Swedish interior from the 1950s.

5 Table Settings

Re-creations of table settings from the 16th to 20th centuries highlight customs about food and drink, and how cutlery and drinking vessels have developed.

3 Main Hall

A fitting entrance to the museum, the huge hall has as centrepiece a monumental pink statue of King Gustav Vasa by Carl Milles carved in 1924, in oak **(right)**.

4 Dolls' Houses

There are 15 dolls' houses, which reflect the styles and home decor of different periods in history.

6 Sámi Life in Sweden

The Sámi are the Nordic countries' only, and Europe's northernmost, indigenous people. This exhibition examines their traditional way of life and influences on Swedish culture.

8 Swedish Folk Art in the 18th and 19th Centuries

Rural folk art blossomed in the 18th and 19th centuries – craftspeople passed on their skills from one generation to the next. Indeed, its heritage lives on today as a big influence on Swedish design **(above)**.

9 Strindberg Collection

The museum owns the largest single collection of August Strindberg's paintings in the world. Sixteen of these are on display, along with photographs taken by Strindberg and several of his original manuscripts.

Nordiska Museet façade

7 Small Objects 1700–1900

From 1872, Artur Hazelius began gathering the items that make up this collection. As he wandered through rural Sweden, Hazelius acquired a complete range of household objects.

Nordiska Museet floorplan

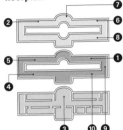

Key to Floorplan
- First floor
- Second floor
- Third floor

10 Power of Fashion – 300 Years of Clothing

This exhibit **(below)** looks at clothing from the 1780s, 1860s and 1960s, all decades when fashion and looks were influenced by the economy, flow of ideas and technical developments.

NEED TO KNOW

Map Q4
- Djurgårdsvägen 6–16
- 08 519 546 00 ■ Tram 7; buses 67, 69 & 76 ■ www.nordiskamuseet.se

Open Sep–May: 10am–5pm daily (till 8pm Wed); Jun–Aug: 9am–6pm daily

Adm 120 kr (adults); under 18s free

■ Borrow an audio guide and follow a map to see the best of the museum in an hour. The guide explores the galleries, as well as the museum's history and architecture. Guides are available in several languages.

■ The museum restaurant serves hot, traditional, Swedish-style meals.

🔟 ⭐ Historiska Museet

The Swedish History Museum, opened in 1943, focuses on early civilization in Sweden, especially from the initial traces of human societies to the Middle Ages. It is particularly renowned for its Gold Room. Built in reinforced concrete to ensure security, the room showcases 52 kg (114 lbs) of gold objects, as well as over 250 kg (551 lbs) of silver items, mainly from the Bronze Age to the Middle Ages. Other sections take a fresh approach of presenting historical trends and events up to the present through engaging displays.

1 Medieval Massacre
With the help of unique objects, such as this rusted armour **(above)**, the horrifying story of the battle between the farmers of Gotland and the well-trained soldiers of the Danish army is told.

2 Maria from Viklau
Wood has long been a popular material for sculptures in Sweden. This richly gilded and colourful figure of the Madonna without child is one of the best-preserved examples of early medieval Swedish sculpture. This piece originates from Viklau Church on the island of Gotland, back in the late 1100s.

3 Gold Room
The priceless artifacts in the Gold Room **(below)** include Bronze Age jewellery and a Medieval reliquary, demonstrating the skills of craftsmen of that era.

Historiska Museet Floorplan

Key to Floorplan
- Lower ground floor
- Ground floor
- First floor

6 History Unfolds

Created by different artists, History Unfolds is a fascinating exhibition detailing Sweden's history and how it has influenced Swedish society. All the artwork is inspired by the museum's collections.

7 Alunda Elk

This carved stone moose head was used as a ceremonial axe; animals such as moose and bear were symbols of the gods in the Stone Age.

8 Bronze Age Finds

Priceless artifacts have been uncovered after 3,000 years, often by amateurs. These include human figures in bronze **(left)** found in Skåne, a gold bowl discovered by an army lieutenant and his daughter out for a walk in 1847, and a gold cup unearthed by a widow in 1859, for which she earned the equivalent of six months' wages.

4 Vikings

The embellished swords of the Vikings are on display here, but shattering many of the myths surrounding the Vikings are objects from everyday life **(above)** that prove that they mostly led a peaceful existence as traders.

5 Medieval Art

This unique exhibition displays decorative ecclesiastical items, such as ornate altarpieces, wood carvings and religious art, from the 12th to the 16th centuries.

BRONZE DOORS

Historiska Museet's bronze doors are called Historiens Portar or 'The Gates of History'. They took Swedish sculptor Bror Marklund 13 years to make and weigh around one ton. Their engravings depict the history of Sweden from the Stone Age to the Middle Ages with one exception – a 1950s pilsner bottle on the right-hand door, a tribute to the workers who built the museum.

9 History of Sweden

Discover Swedish history from the 11th century to the present in a series of displays based around events in the lives of famous and lesser-known historic persons.

10 The Woman from Barum

This moving exhibit features the skeleton of a 155-cm- (5-ft-) tall woman who lived in the Stone Age **(above)**. It tells us that she died at around 45 years of age and that she had borne many children. She was discovered in the 1930s, buried in a pit.

NEED TO KNOW

MAP Q2 ■ Narvavägen 13–17 ■ 08 519 556 00 ■ Tram 7 to Djurgårdsbron; buses 67, 69 & 76; Tunnelbana to Karlaplan ■ www.historiska.se

Open 1 Sept–31 May: 11am–5pm Tue & Thu–Sun, 11–8pm Wed, closed Mon; 1 Jun–31 Aug: 10am–5pm daily; closed for Midsummer

■ Informative audio guides are available in different languages for many of the exhibitions for a small charge.

■ Children of all ages are well catered for here with a number of activities, including a history trail from Viking times through to the Middle Ages, guided tours, special audio guides and themed weekends.

■ Café Rosengården (same opening hours as the museum) serves lunch, snacks and drinks.

TOP 10 ★ Hagaparken

A vast green area north of the city, the historic Haga is one of Stockholm's most beloved parks. Created in the late 18th century by King Gustav III, its natural "English" style was a reaction to formal Baroque designs. Some 26,000 trees were originally planted, interspersed with lawns and winding pathways. Buildings erected between 1786 and 1793 include the Chinese Pavilion, Copper Tents and the Temple of Echo. It is the perfect getaway in any season – in summer, it is popular for picnics, sunbathing or just taking it easy.

1 Stora Pelousen

Epitomizing the park's English character, the *Pelouse* – French for lawn – has been a recreational destination for Stockholmers for over 200 years. It is a popular sunbathing spot in summer, while skiers take over in winter.

2 Cafés

The Copper Tents have a coffee shop and picnic room. A small café in the park serves freshly baked cinnamon buns, coffee and snacks.

3 Echo Temple

A Swedish national monument, this temple **(left)** was built in 1790 as a summer dining room for King Gustav III. It is an outdoor museum and a popular wedding venue.

4 Copper Tents

The tents' façades are adorned with painted copper plates **(above)**, giving the illusion of a sultan's encampment. The middle tent houses the park museum.

MAP G2 ■ 4 km (2.5 miles) N of Stockholm ■ 08 27 42 52 ■ Bus 52 from Slussen, Sergels Torg and various stops in the city (direction Karolinska Sjnkhuset (Hospital) to Haga Norra or Haga Södra); Tunnelbana to Odenplan then bus 515 or 519 ■ www.kungahuset.se

Park: open year round

Butterfly and Bird House: open Apr–Sep: 10am–4pm daily; Oct–Mar: 10am–3pm Tue–Sun; adm: 95 kr (adults), 50 kr (4–15s), family ticket: 260 kr

Haga Parkmuseum: open 10am–3pm Thu–Sun

Gustav III's Pavilion: open

Jun–Aug: Tue–Sun by guided tour only

■ Download a free English audio guide to the park as an MP3 to your audio player or phone from www.onspotstory.com.

■ There are many secluded spots and plenty of park benches to enjoy a picnic.

Map of Hagaparken

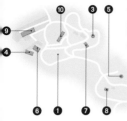

6 Haga Parkmuseum

The original model of the palace that King Gustav III was having built at the time of his assassination in 1792, and which never made it to completion, is on display in the museum. It also includes information about the people associated with Haga, such as the poet Carl Michael Bellman.

LOCAL PERSONALITY

Local composer Carl Michael Bellman (1740–95) was a great favourite of King Gustav III, who founded Hagaparken, and much of Bellman's writing is associated with the park. His most popular song *Fjäriln vingad syns på Haga,* describes the beauty of Hagaparken. It can be recited off by heart by many Swedes.

7 Gustav III's Pavilion

Dating from 1787, this pretty little palace (above) has light, airy interiors, inspired by the antique Roman villas of Pompeii, which had just been discovered.

9 Butterfly and Bird House

Even in the depths of the harsh Swedish winter, the daytime temperature in this tropical rainforest never drops below 25° C (77° F). The house provides a habitat for shimmering butterflies (below), tropical insects, spiders and parrots.

5 Chinese Pagoda

The open octagonal building was built in 1787, its oriental tent roof adorned with dragon heads with bells. It was repaired in 1974, when new dragons made of toughened plastic replaced the former decaying oak ones.

8 Turkish Pavilion

Completed in 1788, this pavilion was used by King Gustav III to hold meetings with his closest advisors. There are plans to restore the original furnishings, which have been traced in the royal palaces.

10 Haga Ruins

Work started on the foundations and cellars of a grand palace in 1786 but ceased when Gustav III was murdered. The palace was never completed (left).

The Top 10
of Everything

**Brick Gothic interior of Storkyrkan,
Stockholm's cathedral**

TOP10 Moments in History

1 **1252: Foundation of Stockholm**

Stockholm is first mentioned in records from the 13th century. The name probably originates from the Swedish words *stock* (log) and *holm* (islet) – for the logs used to build the Gamla Stan area *(see p84–91)*, and particularly the fortress built by the ruler Birger Jarl in 1252. This protected the passage from Lake Mälaren to the Baltic, vital for trade with Germans. It burned down in 1697, and the present-day Royal Palace was built on site.

2 **1520: Stockholm Bloodbath**

The culmination of a long Danish campaign to take control of Sweden, the Stockholm Bloodbath saw around 80–90 people, mainly clergy and members of the nobility who supported the influential Sture party, being executed one by one at Stortorget, outside the Tre Kronor palace. The event led to severe opposition to Danish rule.

3 **1523: King Gustav Vasa**

Having managed to avoid the Stockholm Bloodbath, nobleman Gustav Vasa led a rebellion against Danish rule; it ended with him being crowned king on 6 June 1523 – Sweden's National Day. Sweden was united under his 37-year rule, an era seen as the birth of modern Sweden, during which it also became a Protestant country.

Portrait of Gustav Vasa

4 **1792: Murder of Gustav III**

Gustav III was a patron of the arts, literature and theatre; he founded prestigious academies, such as the Swedish Academy and the Royal Opera, and initiated reform programmes. But opposition to his absolute powers and costly foreign policy cost him his life – in 1792, he was shot during a masked ball at Stockholm's Opera House.

5 **1871: Industrialization**

The completion of a railway to both the north and the south helped Stockholm begin its rapid industrial progress. In 1876, Lars Magnus Ericsson founded the Ericsson phone company in the capital, leading the way for Stockholm to establish an extensive phone network.

6 **1912: Summer Olympics**

The Stockholm Olympic Stadium, built for the 1912 Olympics, is still used as a major sports and concert venue. The games were known as the "Swedish masterpiece" because they were so well organized, and included the first such use of electronic timing and PA systems.

Etching of the Stockholm Bloodbath

7 1936: Rise of the Social Democrats

Dominating Swedish politics from 1936 until the 1980s, the Social Democrats established the modern welfare state and shaped the 20th-century development of Stockholm. Poverty was virtually eradicated in the 1930s and 1940s, and almost the entire country was electrified and connected by new roads.

8 1965: Housing Modernization Programme

A construction project, known as the Million Programme, succeeded in its aim to build over a million new homes, but received mixed reactions – the main criticism being that many of the blocks were uninspiring.

Former Prime Minister Olof Palme

9 1986: Olof Palme's Assassination

The killing of popular Prime Minister Olof Palme in central Stockholm on 28 February 1986 was shocking. Palme was shot while returning from the cinema; his murder has never been solved. The reward for finding the killer stands at €5 million.

10 2000: Into the 21st Century

Present-day Sweden is regarded as having a robust economy and seen as a leader in many technological fields as well as design and style. A strong promoter of equal rights, Sweden consistently ranks high in the OECD Better Life Index.

TOP 10 HISTORICAL FIGURES

Monument to Astrid Lindgren

1 Queen Kristina (1626–89)
Kristina "civilized" a warrior nation by bringing academics and philosophers to Stockholm, before moving to Rome and becoming a Catholic.

2 Carl Linneaus (1707–78)
Responsible for the classification of living things, botanist Linneaus travelled extensively to find different species.

3 Alfred Nobel (1833–96)
This scientist and inventor held 355 different patents, and used his fortune to found the Nobel Prize.

4 August Strindberg (1849–1912)
Author of *The Red Room*, the father of modern Swedish literature was also a playwright, painter and photographer.

5 Tage Erlander (1901–85)
Prime Minister of Sweden for an uninterrupted and unprecedented 23 years, Erlander's tenure is a record for parliamentary democracies.

6 Dag Hammarskjöld (1905–61)
Hammarskjöld was the UN Secretary General from 1953 until his untimely death in a plane crash.

7 Greta Garbo (1905–90)
A Hollywood legend, actress Garbo retired at just 43 years of age.

8 Astrid Lindgren (1907–2002)
An internationally acclaimed author, whose *Pippi Longstocking* series was translated into around 100 languages.

9 Ingmar Bergman (1918–2007)
Director and writer of over 60 films, he was described by Woody Allen as "probably the greatest film artist".

10 Olof Palme (1927–86)
Palme hugely influenced domestic and international politics, and was twice Prime Minister.

🔟 Churches

1 Tyska Kyrkan

This church is a reminder that German merchants dominated the Old Town in the Middle Ages. Also called St Gertrude's Church after the patron saint of travellers, it was founded in 1571, and includes a gallery built in 1672 for German royals. The pulpit from 1660 is in ebony and alabaster *(see p88)*.

Stained-glass window, Tyska Kyrkan

2 Storkyrkan

Stockholm's cathedral, with origins dating back to the 13th century, is known for its collection of artistic treasures. The sculpture *St George and the Dragon* by Bernt Notke, from 1489, was created to mark the Battle of Brunkeberg, while the "Sun Dog Painting" of a light phenomenon over Stockholm in 1535 is said to be the oldest colour depiction of the city *(see p86)*.

3 Högalidskyrkan

MAP B5 ■ Högalids Kyrkväg
■ 08 616 88 00 ■ Open 9am–3pm
Mon–Fri (closed for lunch noon–1pm), 10am–4pm Sat & Sun ■ www.svenskakyrkan.se/hogalid

This National Romantic-style church was completed in 1923. Legend has it that it was financed by two sisters,

each more affluent than the other. One of the octagonal towers appears to be taller when viewed from certain angles, though both towers are in fact 84 m (275 ft) high.

4 Gustav Vasa Kyrka

MAP B2 ■ Odenplan ■ 08 508
886 00 ■ Open 9am–noon Mon–Fri
■ www.svenskakyrkan.se/gustafvasa

The Italian Neo-Baroque-style dome of this church dominates Odenplan square. Built in 1906, the church contains Sweden's largest Baroque sculpture, which forms the altar. It was created by court sculptor Burchardt Precht between 1725 and 1731 for the Uppsala Cathedral.

5 Adolf Fredriks Kyrka

MAP L1 ■ Holländargatan 16
■ 08 20 70 76 ■ Open 9am–noon
Mon–Fri ■ www.svenskakyrkan.se/adolffredrik

Dating from 1768, this city centre church is built in the shape of a Greek cross with a central dome. The interior includes a memorial sculpture to French philosopher Descartes by Johan Tobias Sergel. The cemetery contains the grave of Prime Minister Olof Palme *(see p39)*.

6 Riddarholmskyrkan

The burial church for the Swedish royal family since medieval times, this is one of Stockholm's oldest buildings, with parts of it dating from the 13th century. More of a museum than a church, it is only open to the public in the summer *(see p85)*.

Riddarholmskyrkan

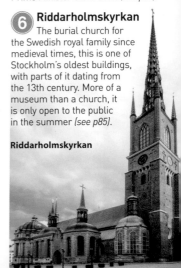

The nave of Sofia Kyrka, showing its National Romantic features

7 Sofia Kyrka
MAP E6 ▪ Vitabergsparken
▪ 08 615 31 00 ▪ Open 9am–5pm
Mon–Fri, 10am–5pm Sat & Sun
▪ www.svenskakyrkan.se/sofia-kyrka

Set high up in Vitabergs park, Sofia
Kyrka was built in 1906 after Gustaf
Hermansson won a contest for its
design. The building has National
Romantic and Gothic influences.

8 Maria Magdalena Kyrka
MAP M6 ▪ Bellmansgatan 13
▪ 08 462 29 40 ▪ Open 9am–noon &
1–3pm Mon, Tue, Thu & Fri; 9am–
noon Wed ▪ www.svenskakyrkan.se/
mariamagdalena

Maria Magdalena began
as a funeral chapel in the
14th century. The current
building, with its pretty
yellow spire, was finished
in 1763. Famous national
poet and singer Evert
Taube is buried here.

9 Katarina Kyrka
MAP D5
▪ Högbergsgatan 13
▪ 08 743 68 00 ▪ Open
11am–5pm Mon–Sat,
10am–5pm Sun ▪ www.
svenskakyrkan.se/katarina

Completed in 1695, this
church was damaged by
fire in 1723 and then
burned down almost
completely in 1990.

It took five years to restore. Its
graveyard is the resting place of
famous Swedes, including assassinated foreign minister Anna Lindh.

10 Engelbrektskyrkan
MAP D1 ▪ Östermalmsgatan
20b ▪ 08 406 98 00 ▪ Open 11am–
3pm Tue–Sun ▪ www.svenskakyrkan.
se/engelbrekt

Opened in 1914, Engelbrektskyrkan
dominates the Lärkstaden area of
Östermalm, with its slim tower and
the highest nave in Scandinavia supported by eight granite pillars. Its
interior features suitably monumental paintings by Olle Hjortzberg.

TOP 10 Museums and Galleries

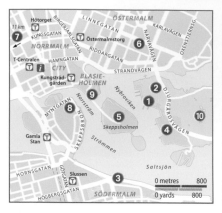

the ages. The museum is housed in a palatial building on Djurgården island (see pp30–31).

3 Fotografiska
Opened in 2010 as a centre for contemporary photography, the gallery presents four large exhibitions and a vast number of smaller ones annually. Housed in a former industrial Jugend-style building on Stockholm's waterfront, it also has an excellent café-bar (see p94).

1 Vasamuseet
The only fully preserved 17th-century warship in the world, the *Vasa*, despite its impressive appearance, sank shortly after setting sail on its maiden voyage in 1628 and was not recovered until 1961. With three masts projecting from the roof, the Vasamuseet is a unique attraction (see pp14–15).

2 Nordiska Museum
Discover Sweden's cultural history in this museum. Exhibitions on trends and traditions, folk art, textiles and fashion, and furnished rooms reveal life in Sweden through

4 ABBA The Museum
Few cultural entities have put Stockholm – and Sweden – on the map like ABBA did in the 1970s and 1980s, when they ruled the global pop charts. See their costumes, gold records and other memorabilia up close, and even try singing along with their 3D holograms at this fun museum – an essential visit for all ABBA fans (see p78).

5 Moderna Museet
This museum contains one of the world's finest collections of 20th-century art, including works by

Moderna Museum on the waterfront

Picasso, Matisse and Dalí, and makes ongoing acquisitions of recent contemporary art. It also houses photographic art and photography, spanning from the 1840s to the present day *(see p86)*.

6 Historiska Museet
The Swedish History Museum brings civilization alive from the earliest settlements to the Middle Ages. Highlights include exhibits about the Vikings, the life of eight different people from prehistory and the Gold Room *(see pp32–3)*.

7 Drottningholm
One of Stockholm's three World Heritage Sites, Drottningholm comprises a perfectly preserved 17th- and 18th-century palace and

Drottningholm palace

gardens. The official residence of the Swedish Royal family, it is nevertheless open to the public; an ideal way to visit in summer is a one-hour boat trip across Lake Mälaren from the city direct to the palace *(see pp24–5)*.

8 The Royal Palace (Kungliga Slottet)
The world's biggest palace still used by a head of state, this splendidly appointed building houses the Royal Apartments, the Hall of State, the Treasury and the Tre Kronor Museum. The magnificent rooms range in style from Rococo to Baroque to Gustavian *(see pp26–7)*.

Renoir at the Nationalmuseum

9 Nationalmuseum
Paintings and sculptures by great masters such as Rembrandt, Renoir, Rubens, Degas and Gauguin and those by Swedish masters Anders Zorn and Carl Larsson are housed in Sweden's national gallery. The museum is under renovation until 2018 – some temporary exhibits are at Kulturhuset Stadsteatern, on Sergels Torg *(see p85)*.

10 Skansen
A collection of buildings from across Sweden, including an entire 19th-century town, is the principal attraction at this open-air museum, concert venue, zoo, playground and park. Traditional crafts, including glassblowing, are practised in the workshops, while the zoo is home to a wide range of Nordic animals, including bears and lynx *(see pp12–13)*.

TOP10 Parks and Gardens

and good views. There is also a pleasant waterside walk from Tanto to Hornstull (see p95).

3 Stora Skuggan
Bus 40 to Stora Skuggan

Located north of the city centre, Stora Skuggan is a popular recreational venue with open areas. In its centre is a youth-run city farm with animals to meet and greet, and a café in an 18th-century building nearby.

4 Vasaparken

Lying between the squares of St Eriksplan and Odenplan, Vasaparken offers many recreational activities. From November to March there is a mechanically frozen ice rink, keeping the ice good at all times (see p73).

5 Kungsträdgården

A lively leafy square very close to the main central shopping areas, Kungsträdgården, or "King's Garden" has numerous cafés and restaurants along its perimeter. Enjoy the pretty "tunnel" of cherry blossom in the spring, concerts in the summer and ice-skating and a Christmas market in the winter (see p66).

1 Hagaparken

A natural English-style landscaped park, Hagaparken is loved for its tree-lined avenues, beautiful lawns and royal buildings. A highlight is the tropical butterfly house, which is also home to exotic birds. Enjoy lunch or a snack inside the blue Copper Tents (see pp34–5).

2 Tantolunden

This park in Södermalm is a popular summer hangout and picnic spot, and includes a few cafés and a mini-golf course. Take a stroll up the hill to enjoy the allotment gardens

Kungsträdgården in bloom

Rosendals Trädgård, Djurgården

⑥ Djurgården
MAP G4 ■ Tram 7 to
Djurgården; get off at Skansen or
the terminus at Waldermarsudde

No trip to Stockholm is complete
without visiting Djurgården. Not only
is it home to several of the city's
major museums and attractions –
notably Skansen *(see pp12–13)* and
Vasamuseet *(see pp14–15)* – but this
royal park is an extensive area of
greenery with excellent walks and
views across the water. Do not miss
Rosendals Trädgård, a garden prac-
tising biodynamic agriculture, with
an excellent café *(see p53)*.

⑦ Skinnarviksparken
MAP B5

Head to this park on a fine day to
picnic with the locals. Featuring a
wonderful view across Riddarfjärden
and of the city, it is ideal for long
summer evenings. The park features
Swedish artist Arne Jones' stainless-
steel sculpture, *Progression*. There
is a small summer café-kiosk and
a playground for the kids.

⑧ Vitabergsparken
MAP E6

This hilly park – whose name means
the White Mountains Park – in
Södermalm includes an open-air
theatre hosting a schedule of free
summer concerts and dance performances of all kinds. At its highest
point is Sofia Kyrka, a church inaugurated in 1906 *(see p41)*. Wooden
workmen's cottages line the park, a
reminder that this trendy area was
once Stockholm's poorest. There is
also one of the city's oldest allotment
gardens, also dating from 1906.

⑨ Bergianska Trädgården
Frescati, 5 km (3 miles) N of
central Stockholm ■ Bus 40 or
540; Tunnelbana Universitetet
■ Conservatory and Orangery:
open 11am–5pm daily; 11am–
4pm in winter ■ Edvard Anderson
Conservatory: adm ■ www.
bergianska.se

Not far from the pretty Brunnsviken
waterside walk, the Bergianska
Botanic Garden dates back to the
18th century but shifted to its current
location in 1885. Tropical plants
bloom in the Orangery and Edvard
Anderson Conservatory, which are
used for research by Stockholm
University. The orangery has a café.

Conservatory, Bergianska Trädgården

⑩ Humlegården
Oak trees and open lawns
characterize this central green oasis
that dates back to the 16th century
when it was the Royal Fruit Garden,
but has been open to the public since
1869. It includes a large playground
and skateboard ramp, and is also
home to the National Library of
Sweden and a large statue of Carl
Linnaeus *(see p39)*. The Debaser
nightclub *(see p51)* has a bar and
restaurant here open from late April
to the end of August *(see p77)*.

Off The Beaten Track

The elegant pool at the Sturebadet

1 Sturebadet
MAP D2 ■ Sturegallerian ■ Open 8am–8pm Mon–Fri, 8am–4pm Sat, 9am–3pm Sun ■ www.sturebadet.se

Dating back to the 19th century and once a haunt of Greta Garbo, plush Sturebadet is one of Stockholm's most upscale swimming pools, gyms and spas. Day passes are available; book treatments well in advance.

2 Fjällgatans Kaffestuga
MAP E5 ■ Fjällgatan 37 ■ Open 9am–5pm Mon–Sun ■ Closed Oct–Mar ■ www.fjallgatan.com

Enjoy a coffee or an ice cream with great panoramic views over all of Stockholm at this summer café and terrace, perched on the edge of the cliffs above Södermalm. It faces out towards Gamla Stan, Djurgården, the archipelago and beyond.

3 Hammarbybacken
Hammarby fabriksväg 111 ■ 02 808 80 61 ■ Open 3–10pm Mon and Fri, 10am–10pm Tue–Thu, 9am–6pm Sat–Sun, winter only ■ www.skistar.com/hammarbybacken

It sounds unlikely, but downhill skiing is possible in the heart of Stockholm. The man-made slope here offers quality floodlit pistes – covered by snow cannon – for skiers of all ages and abilities winter round. Views from the top stretch to Södermalm.

4 Långholmen
MAP A4 ■ www.langholmen.com

Home to one of Sweden's largest prisons for 100 years, the island of Långholmen, just off the north-western tip of Södermalm, is a lush green oasis perfect for walks, picnics and swimming. The prison is now a hotel/hostel and museum (see p117).

5 Korvkiosk Teatern
MAP D6 ■ Ringen centrum ■ Open 11am–9pm Mon–Thu, 11am–10pm Fri–Sat, 11am–8pm Sun ■ www.korvkiosk.se

Sample traditional Swedish street food elevated to a whole new level at this fancy hot dog kiosk, founded by star chef Magnus Nilsson. Try a *tunnbrödsrulle* – a hot dog with mashed potato and shrimp salad, wrapped in a flatbread, and best enjoyed with chocolate milk.

6 Hornstulls Marknad
MAP A5 ■ Hornstulls Strand ■ Open 11am–5pm Sat–Sun ■ Closed Oct–Mar ■ www.hornstullsmarknad.se

Every weekend, the waterfront strip at Hornstull is transformed into an open-air flea market with stalls selling art, antiques, records, crafts and more, and myriad food trucks.

Bric-a-brac stall, Hornstulls Marknad

Lifts ascend the vast Ericsson Globe

7 The Sweden Solar System

Ericsson Globe, Globentorget 2
■ www.swedensolarsystem.se

The world's largest scale model of our solar system has its centre here. The Ericsson Globe (see p101) – the world's largest spherical building – represents the Sun and models of the inner planets, from Mercury to Jupiter.

8 Färgfabriken

Lövholmsbrinken 1
■ **Exhibition hall open 11am–7pm Thu, 11am–4pm Fri, 11am–5pm Sat & Sun** ■ www.fargfabriken.se

Discover Stockholm's thriving art scene at this exhibition and events space set in a 19th-century paint factory. Exhibitions change regularly, so see the website for details.

9 Vinterviken

Between Gröndal and Aspudden ■ www.vinterviken.com

As well as being a picturesque suburban park surrounding a bay in Lake Mälaren, Vinterviken is also renowned as the site of the former laboratory and factory, where, in the mid-19th century, chemist Alfred Nobel (see p39) first produced and tested dynamite. Renovation work in the 1990s transformed the industrial area into the present-day recreational park. One of Nobel's former factory buildings houses the Vinterviken café, restaurant and events venue.

10 Spritmuseum

MAP E4 ■ **Djurgårdsvägen 38** ■ **08 121 313 00** ■ **Open 10am–5pm Mon, 10am–7pm Tue–Sat, noon–5pm Sun** ■ www.spritmuseum.se

With its state-owned off-licences and history of home-distilling illegal moonshine, Sweden has a some-what bittersweet relationship with alcoholic spirits. The Spritmuseum is an offbeat shot of history, culture and strong booze. The great restaurant offers creative local cuisine.

Restaurant at the Spritmuseum

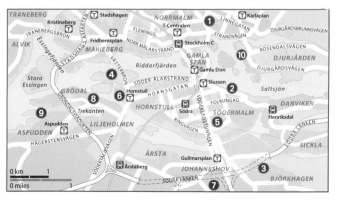

🔟 Children's Attractions

Ice-skaters enjoying the winter rink at Kungsträgården in the city centre

1 Junibacken
MAP Q4 ■ Galärvarvsvägen
■ 08 587 230 00 ■ Tram 7; bus 44
or 69 ■ Open 10am–5pm Tue–Sun
(Jul–Aug: 10am–5pm daily) ■ Adm
■ www.junibacken.se

The storybook world of Junibacken
opens up like a fantasy adventure.
Characters from children's books
live around the Storybook Square,
while the Story Train transports
visitors into the fairytale world of
Swedish author Astrid Lindgren.

Kids' story-themed Junibacken

2 Fjäderholmarna
This island is an ideal kids' day
out. Activities include pottery and
textile printing, climbing a pirate ship
or petting rabbits. There are picnic
and play areas and the path along the
shoreline is stroller friendly (see p16).

3 Ice-Skating Rinks
Kungsträdgården (see p66) in
the city centre, Vasaparken (see p73)
in Vasastan, and Medborgarplatsen
(see p93) on Södermalm all have
outdoor skating rinks in winter.
Several ice-hockey rinks are also
open to the public. Visit the tourist
office for an up-to-date list.

4 Aquaria Vattenmuseum
MAP Q5 ■ Falkenbergsgatan 2
■ 08 660 90 89 ■ Tram 7; bus 44
■ Open 10am–4:30pm Tue–Sun
■ Adm ■ www.aquaria.se

Find out what life is like in a living
Amazon rainforest, with giant catfish,
stingrays and piranhas, at this small
aquarium. Visitors can get close to
sharks and a Baltic exhibit with wild
sea trout spawning indoors. The
café, with views over the harbour,
is a good place to relax.

5 Tekniska museet
MAP G3 ■ Museivägen 7
■ 08 450 56 00 ■ Open 10am–5pm
Thu–Tue, 10am–8pm Wed ■ Adm
■ www.tekniskamuseet.se

Sweden's National Museum of
Science and Technology is packed
with things to entertain and inspire
kids, be it making virtual sculptures
in the MegaMind Zone or marvelling
at Uno Milton's old model railway.

6 Swimming Pools

Hammarby slussväg 20 ▪ 08 508 402 58 ▪ Adm

Eriksdalsbadet, the city's main swimming pool, has adventure pools for children and an outdoor pool in summer. The main adventure pool is comfortably warm and 1.4 m (4.6 ft) deep with two slopes. The outdoor pool is open from late May through to late August.

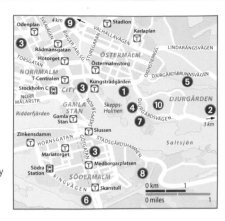

7 Gröna Lund

There are rides and fairground attractions for children of all ages at this traditional funfair. Do not miss the Fun House, the Mirror Pavilion and the various traditional sideshows (see pp28–9).

Roller coaster at Gröna Lund

8 Leksaksmuseet

MAP F6 ▪ Tegelviksgatan 22 ▪ 08 641 61 00 ▪ Bus 2 or 66 ▪ Open 10am–5pm Mon–Fri, 11am–4pm Sat & Sun ▪ Adm ▪ www.leksaksmuseet.se

The museum has functioning model railways and Disney figures from the 1930s. There are thousands of toys from over the centuries – cuddly teddy bears, dolls and dolls' houses dating from as far back as the 16th century, as well as toy boats, cars, aeroplanes and motorbikes.

9 Naturhistoriska Riksmuseet

Come face-to-face with dinosaur skeletons while exploring the history of natural life on earth, and also learn about nature in Sweden and the animals found here by following a discovery trail. There are lots of fun activities to entertain children of all ages, including a smell quiz, memory games and interactive exhibits. The Cosmonova IMAX cinema shows a variety of educational natural science documentaries (see p99).

10 Skansen

Lill-Skansen, the children's zoo, has a fun indoor playground as well as small animal enclosures that younger children will love. There are also kids' activities in the museum's historical buildings (see pp12–13).

Exploring the exhibits at Skansen

🔟 Pubs and Bars

① The Flying Elk
One of the best places in the city to sample the latest and best locally and internationally brewed craft beers, The Flying Elk also does reasonably priced artisanal cuisine. Star chef Björn Frantzén's gastropub is informed both by Swedish tradition and British pub culture (see p91).

Elegant interior at Riche

② Riche
Opened in 1896 with an interior and character inspired by the famous Café Riche in Paris, Riche retains an air of elegance and its menu is based around French-Swedish fusion. The media, fashion and art crowd gather here to listen to unconventional DJ sets from Tuesdays to Saturdays. It is also open for breakfast (see p80).

③ Snotty Sounds Bar
Tiny, snug and low-lit, Snotty's is one of the bars of choice for music-loving Stockholmers. Record sleeves and pictures of punk and indie music legends adorn the walls, and there are DJs most nights of the week. It is packed at peak times, but that is all part of the atmosphere (see p96).

④ Morfar Ginko and Pappa Ray Ray
These are two laid-back venues in one – they are next to each other and under the same ownership. There is great food and a popular cava bar serving tapas from the counter. A secret courtyard is open during the summer (see p96).

⑤ Café Tranan
The cozy bar in the basement of ever-popular restaurant Café Tranan is second home to Vasastan's music-loving crowd and attracts a good selection of DJs. Friendly and unpretentious, it is crowded on weekends but is also an excellent choice as a place with a bit of life on a weekday evening. The fried herring with mashed potatoes has been a constant on the menu at the café since it opened in 1929 (see p74).

⑥ Nya Carnegiebryggeriet
A joint venture between beer brands Brooklyn and Carlsberg, this micro-brewery and adjoining bar/restaurant at Hammarby Sjöstad is popular with craft-beer-loving Stockholmers. Sample one of several unique and delicious brews from Amber Ale to J.A.C.K. IPA, after taking a tour to see how it was made (see p103).

⑦ Kvarnen
One of the few old-style beer halls in the city, Kvarnen serves beer and traditional Swedish food, including good, traditional lunches, in a retro atmosphere. Its adjoining nightclub-bar is by contrast decorated with bright blue and white tiles and chrome. Kvarnen is also

The old-style Kvarnen beer hall

the pub of Hammarby Football Club and gets crowded and very noisy before home matches *(see p96)*.

⑧ Häktet

Hidden away in courtyard off busy Hornsgatan, former prison-turned-bar Häktet (Swedish for "detention") has become the kind of place you want to get locked in. Narrow and winding with a fine kitchen, three bars and a diverse crowd, it is a popular late-night haunt open until 3am Thursday through to Saturday *(see p96)*.

⑨ BrewDog Kungsholmen

The world-beating Scottish craft beer brand's first bar to open in Stockholm was also their first to open outside of the UK, and it is a hotspot for Sweden's beardy hops-lovers. The bar pours all of BrewDog's signature beers, such as the Punk IPA, plus various guest brews, and they serve good food and coffee too *(see p74)*.

⑩ Landet

Situated next to Telefonplan metro station, bar-restaurant and concert/club venue Landet is so much more than just an unusually hip neighbourhood watering hole. Locals come here for discerningly selected beers, fizz, wines and expertly made cocktails. Keep an eye on listings for the upstairs events space, where up-and-coming musicians perform *(see p103)*.

TOP 10 CLUBS AND NIGHTSPOTS

Clubbers at Marie Laveau

1 Marie Laveau
Home to star DJs and some of the city's best-loved club nights.

2 Trädgården
Hammarby Slussväg 2
Summer-only club with live bands, dance floor, bars and food stalls.

3 Debaser
MAP A5 ▪ Hornstulls Strand 4
A waterfront club with live music, international DJs, and a restaurant. The club also hosts concerts.

4 Café Opera
MAP M3 ▪ Karl XII's Torg
Dance-oriented club nights in an elegant 19th-century building. Attracts guests of all ages.

5 Sturecompagniet
MAP D2 ▪ Sturegatan 4
Four halls on two levels, each with its own musical style.

6 Spy Bar
MAP M1 ▪ Birger Jarlsgatan 20
Attracts media folk and serious clubbers and plays everything from funk and alternative disco to rock and pop.

7 Solidaritet
MAP M2 ▪ Lästmakargatan 3
Electronic dance music from top Swedish and international DJs.

8 Fasching
MAP C3 ▪ Kungsgatan 63
A classic jazz, soul, reggae and Latin club that attracts all ages.

9 Berns
MAP N3 ▪ Berzelii Park
Huge dining room and bars, an outdoor terrace, plus international DJs.

10 Under Bron
A mecca for Stockholm's underground clubbing scene every weekend.

🔟 Cafés

1 Johan and Nyström

Those serious about their coffee will love Direct Trade roasters Johan and Nyström's concept store. They will not only get an unbeatable cup of the black stuff, but they can also learn how to make their own great coffee at home with the in-house training facilities. The shop also sells specialist coffee-making equipment imported all the way from Japan (see p96).

2 Saturnus

Everything is big at Saturnus, with steaming bowls of *caffè latte* plus, according to some, the biggest, and among the best, cinnamon buns in town. It also has a wide range of hot food with good lunches and breakfasts – big as well as small. The theme is colourful and French with a New York twist (see p80).

Pastry selection at Saturnus

3 Sosta

Consistently rated by coffee connoisseurs as one of the best espresso bars in the city. Most unusually for Sweden, the baristas at this espresso bar are decked out in a uniform of striped ties and blue shirts. The quality of Sosta's coffee is excellent, and, what's more, there is a fine pastry selection. There is outdoor seating in the summer, but it is often hard to find a place (see p68).

4 Vete-Katten

The "Wheat Cat" opened in 1928 and still looks like an old-fashioned Swedish café. It offers traditional local cakes with lots of marzipan, and different types of buns. While its front entrance is found on the busy central street of Kungsgatan, it also has a quiet courtyard at the back that is open during the summer (see p68).

5 Sturekatten

One of the most famous cafés and bakeries in Stockholm is the grand old "Sture cat", tucked away in an Östermalm apartment building. It has not been redecorated since the early 20th century, and staff in period dress wait on guests who come here to enjoy some of the biggest and best *kanelbulle* (cinnamon buns) to be found in the city (see p80).

6 Petite France

Award-winning bakery and café in the best French tradition, hidden on a side street not far from the waterfront of Lake Mälaren,

..ite France serves great croissants, ..ioches and French bread. The con- ..nental breakfast is a treat here, and ..they also do lunches *(see p74)*.

7 Chokladkoppen

Something of a Stockholm institution, this popular gay-friendly café on Stortorget – Gamla Stan's central square – is best known for its superior cinnamon buns, and, as the name suggests, big steaming cups of hot chocolate. It is a handy stop-off at which to refuel and break up a busy day's sightseeing *(see p90)*.

8 Mellqvist Kaffebar

Artists, students, newspaper cartoonists and young parents frequent this Södermalm institution from dawn until dusk. Kaffebar seems always to be busy whatever the day or time, but it has recently expanded, making it easier to find a seat. People can sit outside throughout the year, thanks to the outdoor heaters. It serves great coffee and terrific *kardemummabullar* (cardamom buns) *(see p96)*.

9 Greasy Spoon

Enjoy breakfast, brunch or lunch with a British twist, from a full English and eggs Benedict to eggs Florentine or eggs pretty much any way you want them. A Bloody Mary is optional. They do not take advance bookings, so set an alarm nice and early or expect to wait in a queue at peak times *(see p96)*.

Brunch offerings at Greasy Spoon

10 Rosendals Trädgård

A summer paradise, these public gardens showcase organic cultivation to the public. Naturally all food served in the café is organically grown on site, and there is also a bakery and a shop. Grab an outdoor table or take your tray to sit under a tree in the apple orchard during spring and summer. Although pricey, it is exceptionally popular at weekends – choose a weekday to avoid the crowds. Check their website for latest opening times *(see p80)*.

Greenhouses with flower shops and a restaurant, Rosendals Trädgård

Restaurants

Sleek and modern Scandinavian design at Mathias Dahlgren

1 Mathias Dahlgren

A visit to this award-winning restaurant in the Grand Hotel is a gastronomic event. The theme is not ostentatious; simplicity combines with great attention to detail. The food is Swedish with global influences on a daily changing menu. Prices match the experience (see p112).

2 Rolfs Kök

This popular restaurant features in the prestigious Michelin guide and serves creative Modern Swedish dishes, such as pork confit with cabbage and beer-braised onions. The outstanding wine list perfectly complements the food (see p69).

Perch with anchovies, Gastrologik

3 Calexico's

Californian-Mexican cuisine is made with organic ingredients at this lively restaurant, adjoining and owned by music venue and club Debaser. Think quesadillas, burritos and tacos packed with fresh ingredients, such as lime, coriander, chilli, hot salsa, avocado, mango and more (see p97).

4 Lilla Ego

Award-winning chefs Tom Sjöstedt and Daniel Räms serve sophisticated seasonal dishes, such as fallow deer with Jerusalem artichokes and pork tartare with red beet purée, at this unpretentious bistro. The exquisite food, along with the restaurant's friendly neighbourhood vibe, is the reason Lilla Ego is fully booked months in advance (see p75).

5 Gastrologik

The food at Gastrologik is so of-the-moment fresh that there are no standard menus – the best local ingredients of the day dictate the dishes instead. The 18-course tasting menu is a gastronomical journey of new Nordic cuisine (see p81).

6 Nytorget Urban Deli

In keeping with the trendy SoFo area, Nytorget Urban Deli has a New York-style atmosphere: it is a restaurant, bar, deli and store all rolled into one. The atmosphere is unpretentious; families with children will feel at home here (see p97).

7 Ekstedt

A star chef famed for his rustic cooking on open fires, Niklas Ekstedt lit the flame under his signature Stockholm restaurant in 2011, and it has burned brightly ever since. Guests can experience set menus of four or six courses, which can feature anything from dried reindeer to birch-fired wild duck (see p81).

8 Meatballs for the People

There are few dishes more synonymous with Sweden than meatballs, and not many restaurants do them better than Meatballs for the People, with no fewer than 14 different varieties including elk, beef and salmon. Enjoy with classic cream sauce and lingonberries or served on top of linguine (see p97).

9 Punk Royale

Off-the-wall Punk Royale is full of mischief, fun, energy and invention. Expect the unexpected here, with dishes such as caviar served with vodka shots and prawn skewers in a plant pot. The set menu promises "over delivery" and "gastronomic decadence" (see p97).

10 Sturehof

Bustling and cool, this classy seafood restaurant with an excellent reputation focuses on Swedish-French home cooking – the menu follows the seasons, complemented by a huge wine list (see p81).

Kerbside dining at Sturehof

TOP 10 SWEDISH FOOD AND DRINK

Traditional Swedish meatballs

1 Swedish Meatballs
The classic Swedish *köttbullar* are made with beef and served with mashed potato and lingonberry jam.

2 Cinnamon Buns
Kanelbulle, the perfect accompaniment to coffee or tea, is found in almost every café in the city.

3 Smörgåsbord
A spread of different hot and cold dishes that varies according to the event or season.

4 Pytt i Panna
A classic Swedish "hash" based around diced, fried potatoes with meat or a vegetarian meat substitute.

5 Semla
A bun filled with almond paste and whipped cream, traditionally eaten around Shrove Tuesday.

6 Västerbotten Cheese
The king of Swedish cheeses is a hard, salty, cow's milk cheese. Also try some mature Prästost or Grevé.

7 Surströmming
Fermented, tinned, raw herring, eaten in August. Very pungent, so the tin must only be opened outdoors.

8 Cloudberries
A delicacy that flourishes only in cold climates. Cloudberry jam is best enjoyed with ice cream or waffles.

9 Must
Non-alcoholic drink with spices, hops and malt, giving it a sweet, beery taste. Swedes drink it mainly at Christmas and Easter.

10 Swedish Beers
Swedish craft-beer culture is on the up; try a brew from one of Sweden's flourishing microbreweries.

🔟 Places to Shop for Scandi Design

1 Granit
MAP D5 ▪ Götgatan 31 ▪ 08 642 10 68 ▪ www.granit.com

Discover clever new ways to arrange, light and decorate the home with the functional and creative homeware from this furnishing shop.

2 Design House Stockholm
MAP D3 ▪ Hamngatan 18–20 ▪ 08 762 81 19 ▪ www.designhouse stockholm.com

Browse interior design products, porcelain and clothing by top Swedish designers at this chain's flagship shop at the NK department store.

3 Marimekko
MAP D3 ▪ Norrmalmstorg 4 ▪ 08 440 32 75

This Finnish brand's boldly colourful patterns are famous throughout the world. Their largest store stocks clothing, accessories and homeware in new and classic designs.

4 Swedish Hasbeens
MAP E5 ▪ Nytorgsgatan 36a ▪ 08 702 01 01 ▪ www.swedish hasbeens.com

Head here for bold and beautiful women's clogs, handmade using sustainable materials, and based on original Swedish 1970s designs. This is the flagship store of this fashion sensation, in trendy SoFo.

Objects for sale at Designtorget

5 Designtorget
MAP D5 ▪ Götgatan 31 ▪ 08 644 16 78 ▪ www.designtorget.se

Brighten up your life with a smart piece of design from this emporium stocking all kinds of easy-on-the-eye items, primarily by Scandinavian designers. Some well-known brands are stocked, from String shelves to Marianne Westman kitchenware.

6 Svenskt Tenn
MAP E3 ▪ Strandvägen 5 ▪ 08 670 16 98 ▪ www.svenskttenn.se

Swedish-Austrian architect and designer Josef Frank designed the gorgeously patterned and coloured

Bold homeware at Svenskt Tenn

fabrics and furniture sold here. Their waterfront headquarters since 1927 also has a tea room and a studio.

⑦ Fillipa K
MAP D2 ■ Grev Turegatan 18 ■ 08 545 888 88 ■ www.filippa-k.com

Founded in Stockholm in 1993, Filippa Knutsson's fashion brand is an international success story. The latest collections are on display at this flagship store.

⑧ Whyred
MAP D3 ■ Mäster Samuelsgatan 3 ■ 08 660 01 70 ■ www.whyred.com

Designer Roland Hjort's colourful clothing for men and women combines clean lines, neat shapes and quirky details, and is influenced by music and art as much as fashion. Located in plush Östermalm, this is Whyred's flagship store.

Scandi design pieces at Grandpa

⑨ Grandpa
MAP A3 ■ Fridhemsgatan 43 ■ 08 643 60 81 ■ www.grandpa.se

The quality of the product is always more important than the strength of the brand at Grandpa, which stocks a hand-picked selection of fashion, interior and design items.

⑩ Acne Studios
MAP D3 ■ Norrmalmstorg 2 ■ 08 611 64 11 ■ www.acnestudios.com

From the 100 pairs of jeans made by co-founder Jonny Johansson in 1997 and given out to friends, Acne Studios has become an internationally successful fashion house designing both men's and women's collections.

TOP 10 SCANDI ITEMS TO BUY

Brightly coloured Dala horses

1 Dala Horse
Classic Swedish ornaments, these delightful handmade and painted wooden horses come in various sizes.

2 String Pocket Shelving
Take home a suitcase-friendly sized set of one the most iconic of Swedish home furnishings.

3 Harri Koskinen Block Lamp
A simple light bulb "frozen" in a block of glass – a timeless Finnish design.

4 Sandqvist Backpack
Classic-looking, uncomplicated and functional backpacks made with stylish fabric. These and the leather bags have distinct Swedish heritage.

5 Trull Chopping Board
This chopping board, inspired by Lisa Larson's iconic porcelain feline, makes kitchen work more fun.

6 Iittala Candleholder
Simple and elegant Finnish-designed candleholders in various colours for lighting long winter nights.

7 Aretta Dress
A black-and-white striped cotton dress for all occasions by Finland's finest design studio, Marimekko.

8 Acne Jeans
Stockholm's most famous denim export – these cool, comfortable jeans are cut just how they should be.

9 RAINS
Lightweight, fashionable and, most importantly, waterproof Danish raincoats, bags and accessories.

10 Berså Coffee Set
Stig Lindberg's famous floral cup and saucer design made by Gustavsbergs Porslinsfabrik of Sweden. The design has been popular since 1961.

🔟 Stockholm For Free

① Guided Tours of the Swedish Parliament

MAP D4 ■ Helgeandsholmen ■ 08 786 40 00 ■ Open mid-Sep–Jun ■ English tours: 1:30pm Sat & Sun ■ www.riksdagen.se

Take a free guided tour of the Swedish parliament building, the Riksdag. Learn about the work and history of the building and find out what is happening in the parliament today.

② Art in the Underground
Stockholm's Tunnelbana metro system is known as "the world's longest art gallery". Many stations contain artworks, from sculptures and paintings to video installations, all of them free to view. Some stations are artworks in their entirety – such as Solna Centrum, where the raw bedrock of the ceiling is dramatically painted fiery red.

③ Clubbing for Free
Some Stockholm nightclubs and late-night bars offer free entry before a certain hour, typically midnight or sometimes earlier. Debaser (see p51) is particularly well known for this – there may even be a free concert included in the bargain, too.

④ Drottningholm Gardens
At the sprawling royal residency of Drottningholm (see pp24–5) it is free to explore the beautifully manicured Baroque gardens and the Guard's Tent – more than enough for a morning or afternoon's visit.

Swimmers on Långholmen Canal

⑤ Take a Swim
Stockholm's waterways are not only beautiful to look at, but they are also so clean that swimming is possible right in the middle of town. On warm days, beaches, jetties and cliffs are packed with bathers.

⑥ Museums for Free
Many of Stockholm's best museums are free to enter. These include Moderna Museet (see p86), National Museum (see p43), Medelhavsmuseet (see p66) among several others.

⑦ Contemporary Art and Design
Like many of the museums, several contemporary art galleries and exhibitions spaces are free to enter. For example Bonniers Konsthall (see p72) and ArkDes centre for architecture and design (see p88).

Beautiful gardens at Drottningholm

⑧ Explore the Royal Palace Vaults at the Livrustkammaren

MAP D4 ■ Slottsbacken 3 ■ 08 402 30 30 ■ Open 11am–5pm Tue–Sun (till 8pm Thu) ■ Closed Mon ■ www. livrustkammaren.se

Housed in spectacular vaults beneath the Royal Palace (see pp26–7), the Livrustkammaren (Royal Armoury) is the oldest museum in Sweden. It contains arms and armour, robes from royal weddings and coronations and even blood-stained garments worn by royals at their death.

⑨ Camping on the Archipelago

Allemansrätten enshrines in Swedish law everyone's right to roam and to pitch a tent on most public and private land, making wild camping a great way to explore the Stockholm Archipelago (see pp16–19). Facilities such as fresh water and toilets are available for free or at a small price at some designated camping spots.

⑩ Concerts and Festivals for Free

Fritz's Corner: www.fritzscorner.se ■ Popaganda: www.popaganda.se

Discover the Stockholm music scene which has produced many world-renowned acts at free shows and concerts staged at Fritz's Corner and the free annual festival Popaganda at Parkteatern.

TOP 10 BUDGET TIPS

Flea market, Blasieholmstorg

1 Look out for *loppis*, or flea markets. They can be great for finding bargain Scandi design gems.

2 Central Stockholm is compact and very pretty, so try to walk around as much as possible.

3 Many restaurants and cafés do a very reasonably priced all-inclusive midday deal, known as a *dagens* lunch.

4 Make like a Swede and save money by having a pre-party before heading on a night out.

5 Know your alcohol pricing: spirits and cocktails are particularly expensive in Sweden. It is not common to buy rounds of drinks.

6 Pack a picnic and head for one of Stockholm's many parks or beaches, or the archipelago.

7 An SL Access card (see p106) includes trips on the Djurgården ferries – great for city views from the water.

8 You can ice skate for free on a frozen Lake Mälaren if the ice is thick enough.

9 Save money on transport by hiring a City Bike (see p107) and using Stockholm's handy cycle lanes.

10 For 250 kr, the Gröna Kortet ticket grants daily free admission to Gröna Lund amusement park and all concerts all season long.

Carousel at Gröna Lund

🔟 Festivals and Events

1 Stockholm Fashion Week
www.fashionweek.se

The Swedish Fashion Council stages fashion events each year – January/February and August see the major fashion weeks. Other related activities organized during the season include exhibitions, trade fairs and press events.

2 Stockholm Marathon
www.stockholm marathon.se

Attracting runners from around the world, this marathon takes place on the last Saturday in May or the first in June, and ends in the Olympic Stadium.

Stockholm Culture Festival

3 Stockholm Music and Arts
www.stockholmmusicandarts.com

Taking place in late July since 2012 in the stunning surrounds of leafy Skeppsholmen, Stockholm Music and Arts is the city's biggest music festival. It always welcomes big-name headliners – past performers include Björk, Prince, Patti Smith and Kraftwerk, to name a few.

Participants in Stockholm Pride

4 Stockholm Culture Festival
www.kulturfestivalen.stockholm.se

Held in August, this festival hosts performances and acts such as dance, music and mime on streets, squares and stages throughout the centre. There is a mini children's festival where kids can dance, sing and listen to stories.

5 Midnattsloppet
www.midnattsloppet.com

The "Midnight Race" is run over 10 km (6 miles) by 24,000 runners from around 9:30pm in Södermalm in mid-August; people run well into the night. There are 16 starting groups, ensuring that all ability levels are catered for, from the serious to those in outrageous fancy dress.

6 Stockholm Pride
www.stockholmpride.org

The Pride Parade, with over 50,000 participants, is the highlight of the week-long gay pride festival held at the end of July or beginning of August. The parade is a celebration of human rights and openness; other events include Pride Park, featuring concerts and stalls.

Stockholm Bauhaus Athletics event

⑦ Stockholm Bauhaus Athletics

www.diamondleague-stockholm.com

The largest annual sporting event in Sweden, Stockholm Bauhaus Athletics is an international track and field event in mid-August. Taking place at the 1912 Olympic Stadium, it is part of the International Association of Athletics Federations' Diamond League – the world's foremost one-day athletic meeting circuit.

⑧ Popaganda

www.popaganda.se

Stockholm's biggest pop festival is held at Eriksdalsbadet's outdoor baths (see p41) over two days at the end of August and focuses on indie pop with a mix of well-established and newer artists.

⑨ Stockholm International Film Festival

www.stockholmfilmfestival.se

Inaugurated in 1990, this two-week-long event in mid-November hosts film screenings all around the city, with an emphasis on new and upcoming, local and international directors. Other highlights through the year include a smaller, five-night outdoor film festival in August.

⑩ Nobel Day

On 10 December which is the anniversary of Alfred Nobel's death, the Nobel Prize is awarded in Stockholm in Physics, Chemistry, Medicine, Literature and Economics. After the award ceremony, a widely telecast banquet with 1,300 guests is held in the Stadshuset (see pp22–3).

TOP 10 NATIONAL HOLIDAYS AND CELEBRATIONS

1 Easter
Traditions include egg painting and consumption of sweets and chocolate hidden in paper eggs.

2 Walpurgis Night, 30 April
A traditional spring festival, Valborg is marked with bonfires and parties.

3 International Workers' Day, 1 May
A national holiday marked by the Social Democratic party and labour groups marching in the city centre.

4 Ascension Day, June
Since this falls on a Thursday, many workers take a klämdag (a day off) on Friday for a long weekend.

5 National Day, 6 June
A public holiday since 2005, this day marks the date of King Gustav Vasa's ascension to the throne.

6 Midsummer's Eve, June
One of the year's biggest holidays, on the Friday closest to 21 June. Skansen is a great place to join in the summer solstice celebrations.

7 Crayfish Season, August
Always popular crayfish parties involve shelling the fish by hand and drinking plenty of schnapps.

8 Lucia, 13 December
White-robed girls sing traditional Christmas songs in candlelit processions at schools, churches and workplaces; saffron buns are eaten.

9 Christmas, 24–26 December
Families gather on Christmas Eve to celebrate with a julbord, the Christmas equivalent of a smörgåsbord.

10 New Year's Eve, 31 December
Locals spill out onto the streets a few minutes before midnight to enjoy fireworks displays around the city.

Crayfish, crispbread and schnapps

Stockholm
Area by Area

Visitors filling Stortorget, a square
bordered by colourful buildings

TOP 10 Norrmalm and City

Considered the central part of town and known as the "City", much of Norrmalm was laid out in the 1960s and 1970s, when a great many of its 18th-century buildings were demolished and replaced with modern high-rise blocks – a move that many people still think was hasty and ill-considered. However, Norrmalm has brightened up in recent years, some areas are pedestrianized, and it is now the place for affordable shopping, with many large, trendy chain stores. Of these, Åhléns City is the largest department store in Sweden, while NK is the most exclusive. The district also has some pleasant squares and the ever-popular Kungsträdgården, an outdoor space where there is always something going on.

Glass obelisk, Sergels Torg

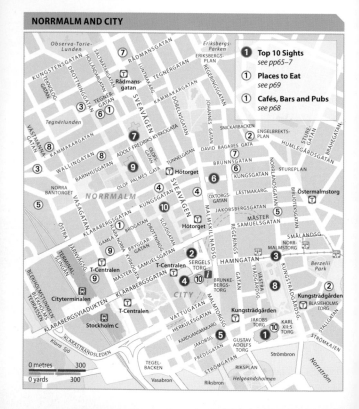

NORRMALM AND CITY

1 **Top 10 Sights**
see pp65–7

1 **Places to Eat**
see p69

1 **Cafés, Bars and Pubs**
see p68

0 metres 300
0 yards 300

Kungliga Operan auditorium

1 Kungliga Operan
MAP M4 ■ Gustav Adolf Torg 2
■ 08 791 44 00 ■ www.operan.se

The Royal Swedish Opera is the country's national stage for opera and ballet. Some productions are performed in their original language such as English, German or Italian (with Swedish subtitles). From August to May there are guided tours in English every Saturday. Take a peek backstage, visit the Royal Suite and look down into the orchestra pit.

2 Sergels Torg
MAP L3

Although not the most beautiful square in Stockholm, Sergels Torg has become an iconic landmark. It is the central hub of the city and home to the T-Centralen Tunnelbana station, where the red and green lines intersect with the blue. The square was designed in the 1960s as part of the modernization of the city centre. It is known for its checkerboard

pedestrian area, which is frequently a venue for public demonstrations and street performances. Its highlight, a glass obelisk, is lit up at night.

3 Hamngatan
MAP M3

Stretching from Sergels Torg to Berzelii Park, Hamngatan is one of Stockholm's top shopping streets. It is home to the classic NK department store, trendy Gallerian and the flagship H&M store. Trams on the number 7 line roll down Hamngatan to Djurgården via Norrmalmstorg. This is also where heritage trams leave for Djurgården (see pp76–81). Norrmalmstorg is the site of the 1973 bank robbery that coined the term "Stockholm Syndrome", in which hostages start to sympathize with their captors.

4 Kulturhuset
MAP L3 ■ Sergels Torg ■ 08 508 315 08 ■ Opening hours vary for different sections and exhibitions ■ Adm fees for events and temporary exhibitions ■ www.kulturhuset. stockholm.se

This cultural centre was designed by architect Peter Celsing as a "cultural living room". It hosts photographic and art exhibitions, films, theatre and much more. Concerts are held indoors, and, in summer, on the rooftop terrace with great views over the city. There is a café and a children's library, and the Stockholm Visitor Center is located inside.

Kulturhuset on Sergels Torg

Greek busts in the Medelhavsmuseet

5 Medelhavsmuseet
MAP M4 ▪ Fredsgatan 2 ▪ 08 519 553 80 ▪ Open noon–8pm Tue–Thu, noon–5pm Fri & Sun ▪ Adm ▪ www.varldskulturmuseerna.se/medelhavsmuseet ▪ Bagdad Café: open from 11:30am Mon–Fri; Jun–Aug: closed Mon

The Museum of Mediterranean and Near East Antiquities has a fine collection of ancient and historical relics from the region. The Egyptian exhibition includes mummies, sarcophagi and other ancient burial finds. The Near East and Islamic collections showcase Islamic art from the 7th century onwards. The Cyprus collection comprises ancient objects excavated by the Swedish Cyprus expedition of 1927–31. The museum has a restaurant called Bagdad Café.

6 Kungsgatan
MAP M2

"King's Street" was built in 1904–5 to connect Kungsholmen, Norrmalm

Cherry blossoms, Kungsträdgården

and Östermalm. It is notable for its two "skyscrapers", Kungstornen, built in 1924–5, and clearly modelled on the Lower Manhattan skyscrapers of that era – they were the first of their kind in Europe. Kungsgatan is a lively shopping street, with many fashion, household and electrical stores, particularly on its eastern end between Hötorget and Stureplan as well as the Rigoletto cinema, dating from 1939.

7 Olof Palme's Plaque and Grave
MAP L1

At the junction of Sveavägen and Tunnelgatan there is a memorial plaque at the spot where Swedish Prime Minister Olof Palme was assassinated on 28 February 1986. People often lay flowers here, particularly on the anniversary of his death. The street to the west was renamed Olof Palmes Gata in his honour. Palme is buried in the nearby Adolf Fredriks Kyrka (see p40), his grave marked by a simple headstone.

8 Kungsträdgården
MAP M3

One of the most popular meeting places in the city, the "King's Garden" is a hive of activity throughout the year. In winter, it hosts a charming Christmas market and is one of the city's most popular venues for ice-skating; during the summer, it is a great place simply to relax. Open-air concerts and other events are held throughout the

year. A park redevelopment planted 285 linden trees, which replaced old and sick elm trees, and new pavilions with cafés, bars and restaurants (see p44).

9 Centralbadet

MAP L1 ■ Drottninggatan 88 ■ 08 545 213 00 ■ Open 7am–9pm Mon–Fri, 9am–9pm Sat, 9am–6pm Sun ■ Adm ■ www.centralbadet.se

Located in a beautiful Art Nouveau building from 1904, Centralbadet is a relaxing oasis just off the busy Drottninggatan. A swimming pool, sun roof, gym, bar, restaurant and the baths are just some of the facilities here. There is also a sauna and a wide range of massages, zone therapy and facial treatments.

Swimming pool in the Centralbadet

10 Hötorget

MAP L2

Just off busy Kungsgatan lies cobbled Hötorget (Hay Market) square, a fruit and vegetable market right in the commercial heart of the city. A statue by sculptor Carl Milles stands outside the pale blue Royal Concert Hall (Konserthuset). To the south stands Filmstaden Sergel, one of the largest multiscreen cinemas in Stockholm showing international blockbusters in their original languages. Beneath the cinema is the Hötorgshallen indoor market, with its vast, mouthwatering displays of Swedish and foreign delicacies. To the north of the square is the excellent Kungshallen food court (see p66).

A DAY IN NORRMALM AND CITY

▶ MORNING

Start the day at Kungsträdgården Tunnelbana – the terminus of the blue line. It is worth a visit, as it is decorated with relics from 18th-century buildings that were torn down in the 1960s. Take the exit at **Kungsträdgården** park; a stroll northwards through the park leads directly to **Hamngatan** (see p65), where the NK department store sports an iconic revolving neon clock on its roof. Carrying on up Hamngatan, there is both Gallerian and the H&M flagship store, before the street opens out on to **Sergels Torg** (see p65). Pop into **Kulturhuset** (see p65) to check out what is on offer and for a coffee at the fifth-floor Café Panorama. Directly off Sergels Torg, pedestrianized Sergelgatan leads to **Hötorget**; grab a light lunch here at either **Hötorgshallen** or **Kungshallen** foodhalls.

AFTERNOON

Not far from Hötorget is **Olof Palme's Plaque**, and his grave in **Adolf Fredriks Kyrka** (see p40), where there is also a memorial to influential French philosopher René Descartes who died in Stockholm in 1649, during his sojourn with Queen Kristina. Spend some time browsing the many shops on **Kungsgatan**, with its 1920s twin towers. From there, walk to **Vete-Katten** (see p68) for traditional fika (coffee and pastries). From the junction of Kungsgatan and Sveavägen, it is not far to **Smak** (see p69) for a good-value dinner.

See map on p64

Cafés, Bars and Pubs

An impressive selection of cakes and Swedish pastries at Vete-Katten

1 Vete-Katten
MAP K2 ■ Kungsgatan 55
■ 08 20 84 05 ■ Open 7:30am–8pm
Mon–Fri, 9:30am–7pm Sat & Sun

An old-fashioned café opened in 1928, the "Wheat Cat" specializes in traditional cakes and buns.

2 Vassa Eggen
MAP D2 ■ Birger Jarlsgatan 29
■ 08 21 61 69 ■ Open 11:30am–2:30pm & 5:30–11pm Mon–Thu, 11:30am–2:30pm & 5:30pm–2am Fri, 5:30pm–2am Sat

A popular grill restaurant, this is also a busy nightspot with DJs until late.

3 Monks Café and Brewery
MAP L1 ■ Sveavägen 39 ■ 08 24 13 10

Not only does this pub stock a vast range of beers, it also brews its own.

4 Kungshallen
MAP L2 ■ Kungsgatan 44
■ 07 086 556 20 ■ Open 9am–11pm Mon–Fri, 11am–11pm Sat, noon–11pm Sun

Hötotorget's food court offers a wide choice of international cuisines.

5 Bianchi Café & Cycles
MAP M2 ■ Norrlandsgatan 20
■ 08 611 21 00 ■ Open 7:30am–7pm Mon–Tue, 7:30am–9pm Wed–Thu, 11am–9pm Sat, 11:30am–5pm Sun

It is all about traditional Italian quality in this café and bicycle shop serving excellent coffee and snacks.

6 Kåken
MAP M2 ■ Regeringsgatan 66
■ 08 20 60 10 ■ Open 6pm–2am Wed–Sat

A trendy American-style bar, this is a good spot for an early evening drink, as it gets busy after work hours.

7 Sosta
MAP L1 ■ Sveavägen 84 ■ 08 612 13 49 ■ Open 8am–6pm Mon–Fri, 10am–5pm Sat

The authentic Italian espressos in this café bar attract rave reviews from Stockholm's coffee aficionados.

8 Pizza Hatt
MAP K1 ■ Upplandsgatan 9
■ Open 1am–9pm Tue–Sun

Sourdough pizzas using only fresh ingredients are served at this quirky place. Eat in or take away.

9 Icebar by Icehotel
MAP C3 ■ Nordic C Hotel, Vasaplan 4 ■ 08 50 56 35 20 ■ Open 4:30pm–midnight Sun–Thu, 3:45pm–1am Fri–Sat

Everything from the interior to the glasses are made out of sculpted ice from the arctic Torne River.

10 Café Panorama
MAP L3 ■ Sergels Torg 3 ■ 08 21 10 35 ■ Open 11am–8pm Tue–Fri, 11am–6pm Sat, 11am–5pm Sun

On the fifth floor of Kulturhuset (see p65), this café lives up to its name with great views over the city.

See map on p64

Places to Eat

PRICE CATEGORIES

For a three-course meal for one with half
a bottle of wine (or equivalent meal),
taxes and extra charges.

ⓚ under 700 kr ⓚⓚ 700–1,000 kr
ⓚⓚⓚ over 1,000 kr

① Supper
MAP K1 ▪ Tegnérgatan 37
▪ 08 23 24 24 ▪ Open 4pm–midnight
Mon–Wed, 5pm–1am Thu–Sat ▪ ⓚⓚ
Various South American flavours
dominate the dishes, which are
meant to be shared.

② Wedholms Fisk
MAP N3 ▪ Nybrokajen 17
▪ 08 611 78 74 ▪ Open 11:30am–2pm
& 6pm–11pm Mon, 11:30am–11pm
Tue–Fri, 5pm–11pm Sat ▪ ⓚⓚ
Traditional, classy fish restaurant
offering a great choice of dishes.

③ Grill
MAP C2 ▪ Drottninggatan 89 ▪
08 31 45 30 ▪ Open 11am–1am Mon–
Fri, 4pm–1am Sat, 3–9pm Sun ▪ ⓚⓚ
This stylish restaurant serves a wide
variety of wood-fired and charcoal-
grilled meats.

④ Smak
MAP L2 ▪ Oxtorgsgatan 14
▪ 08 22 09 52 ▪ 11:30am–2pm & 7pm–
midnight Mon–Thu, 11:30am–2pm &
5pm–1am Fri, 5pm–1am Sat
▪ ⓚⓚ
The concept is simple but
novel at Smak: choose three,
five or seven tasting dishes
and enjoy the combinations.

⑤ Cloud Nine Food and Cocktails
MAP J2 ▪ Torsgatan 1 ▪ 08 653
69 90 ▪ Open Lunch: 11:30am–
2pm Mon–Fri; Dinner: 5–11pm
Mon–Wed, 5pm–midnight
Thu–Sat ▪ ⓚⓚ
Relaxed atmosphere and
French-Asian cuisine; there
is outdoor dining in summer.

⑥ Rolfs Kök
MAP C2 ▪ Tegnérgatan 41
▪ 08 10 16 96 ▪ Open 11:30am–1am
Mon–Fri, 5pm–1am Sat ▪ ⓚⓚ
Enjoy modern interpretations of
classic Swedish dishes in a relaxed,
contemporary setting. Excellent
wine list.

⑦ Nalen Restaurang
MAP M1 ▪ Regeringsgatan 74
▪ 08 505 292 01 ▪ Open 11am–3pm &
4–11pm Mon–Fri, 5–11pm Sat ▪ ⓚⓚ
Serves classic Swedish food.

⑧ Tjabba Thai
MAP K1 ▪ Wallingatan 7
▪ 08 21 99 88 ▪ Open 11am–10pm
Mon–Fri, 2–10pm Sat–Sun ▪ ⓚ
Some of the city's best Thai food is
served here, including good seafood.

⑨ Belgobaren
MAP K3 ▪ Bryggargatan 12a
▪ 08 24 66 40 ▪ Open Lunch: 11am–
2pm; Dinner: from 4pm ▪ ⓚⓚ
Mussels are served in 10 ways, from
classic *moules frites* to those with
Asian curry sauces.

⑩ Operakällarens Bakfickan
MAP M3 ▪ Karl XII:s torg ▪ 08
676 58 00 ▪ Open 11:30am–11pm
Mon–Fri, noon–10pm Sat ▪ ⓚⓚ
This is a place to enjoy traditional
Swedish favourites such as meatballs.

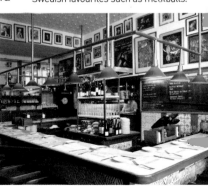
Bar-top seating at Operakällarens Bakfickan

TOP10 Kungsholmen and Vasastan

Once known as "famine island", with grim industrial businesses and cramped housing, Kungsholmen began to improve in the early 20th century when the Stadshuset was built. Today it offers a pleasant alternative to the city centre, with a good variety of shops and cafés. Nearby Vasastan is home to the lively area around Odengatan, with its restaurants, bars and nightclubs as well as the iconic Stadsbiblioteket and the popular Vasaparken.

Stadshuset, seen from Gamla Stan

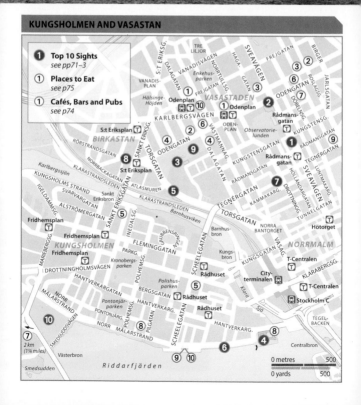

KUNGSHOLMEN AND VASASTAN

❶ **Top 10 Sights**
see pp71–3

① **Places to Eat**
see p75

① **Cafés, Bars and Pubs**
see p74

1 Sveavägen

Broad, straight and linking the city centre with Odenplan and beyond, Sveavägen is built like a classic Parisian boulevard. After an unpromising start at Sergels Torg, the street comes into its own after Hötorget – lined with trees and many upmarket shops along with bars and restaurants. Adolf Fredriks Kyrka *(see p40)* and the Stadsbiblioteket are here. After Odenplan, Sveavägen runs on out to the city's northern fringes, just a short walk from Hagaparken *(see pp34–5)*.

Rooftop of Sven-Harrys Konstmuseum

3 Sven-Harrys Konstmuseum

MAP B2 ▪ Eastmansvägen 10
▪ 08 511 600 60 ▪ Open 11am–7pm Wed–Fri, 11am–5pm Sat & Sun
▪ www.sven-harrys.se

Building contractor and art collector Sven-Harry Karlson built this spectacular, modern, brass-clad building to house exhibition galleries, an art museum, and restaurants, as well as private apartments. The recessed penthouse is a replica of his own 18th-century mansion and displays his art collection. Do not miss the rooftop sculpture garden.

2 Stadsbiblioteket

MAP C1 ▪ Sveavägen 73
▪ 08 508 310 60 ▪ Open 9am–9pm Mon–Thu, 9am–7pm Fri, noon–4pm Sat–Sun ▪ www.biblioteket. stockholm.se

The Stockholm Public Library was one of the most influential buildings constructed in Stockholm in the early 20th century. Opened in 1928, it was designed by Gunnar Asplund in the so-called Nordic Classicist style. Painted in eye-catching pale orange, its highlight is the central rotunda. Inside, packed bookshelves cover the walls of its tiered balconies, yet with its tall, white ceiling, the rotunda is bright and well lit. It was the first public library in Sweden to adopt the principle of open shelves, where books could be accessed without help from the library staff.

4 Stadshuset

With its dramatic waterside setting on Riddarfjärden, the City Hall is visible from far away, and is one of Stockholm's most famous landmarks. It is built from 8 million bricks in the National Romantic style and is home to the municipal council *(see pp22–3)*.

Floor-to-ceiling bookcases in the central rotunda of the Stadsbiblioteket

SHOPPING ON KUNGSHOLMEN

Kungsholmen is a great shopping alternative to the city centre crowds. St Eriksgatan and Fleminggatan are the main shopping streets, while Fridhemsgatan and Hantverkargatan are good for second-hand shops.

The modern Bonniers Konsthall

5 Bonniers Konsthall

MAP B2 ■ Torsgatan 19 ■ 08 736 42 48 ■ Open noon–8pm Wed, noon–5pm Thu–Sun ■ www.bonniers konsthall.se

An unmissable triangular-shaped building designed by local architect Johan Celsing and opened in 2006 contains Bonniers Konsthall, one of Stockholm's leading galleries for both Swedish and international contemporary art. An independent and not-for-profit institution with a mission to increase public consumption of art, it holds free exhibitions that can feature anyone from Turner Prize winners to emerging talent.

6 Norr Mälarstrand

MAP J4

The walk along Norr Mälarstrand is picturesque and popular. Its quay, lined with old ships and houseboats, transforms into a waterside footpath along its western stretch. Either start at Stadshuset or walk towards it from Västerbron (bus 4 stops at Västerbroplan; take the steps down into Rålambshov park to pick up the shoreline walk). Along the way there are several good refreshment and food stops, as well as great views across Riddarfjärden towards Söder.

7 Strindbergsmuseet

MAP K1 ■ Drottninggatan 85 ■ 08 411 53 54 ■ Open noon–4pm Tue–Sun; Jul–Aug: 10am–4pm ■ Adm ■ www.strindbergsmuseet.se

Considered the father of modern Swedish literature, and also a prolific artist, August Strindberg lived in what he called the "Blue Tower" for the last four years of his life. The house is faithfully preserved as he left it, and Strindberg's study, living room and bedroom take visitors back to 1912. There are also many photographic portraits of Strindberg and his family, as well as photographs of places associated with him.

8 Rörstrandsgatan

MAP A2

The street takes its name from the medieval town of Rörstrand, though it is affectionately called "Little Paris" by the residents. Rörstrandsgatan is full of small, interesting stores, which sell everything from British tweed and Italian tiles to handmade chocolates and craft beer. There are also many outdoor cafés and restaurants that give the street a colourful atmosphere during summer. Rörstrandsgatan stretches from S:t Eriksplan to Karlberg Station, and then merges with Karlbergsvägen.

Football pitches in Vasaparken

9 Vasaparken
MAP B2

Vasastan's green lung was developed in the early 20th century as an "open place for free games" – a role it retains today with football pitches, *boules* courts, a landscaped playground and an ice-skating rink in winter. There are also large grassy areas and a popular playground. In 1917, *Arbetaren* (The Worker), a statue by Gottfrid Larsson, was erected to honour the working class. There are numerous kiosks around the park that sell snacks and drinks.

10 Rålambshovsparken
MAP A3

Known locally as "Rålis", this was created as a functional park in 1936, at the same time that Västerbron was built. It is a popular summer haunt with sunbathers, as well as football, *brännboll* (a local form of rounders) and frisbee players. An open-air theatre opened here in 1953.

Norr Mälarstrand on the Kungsholmen waterfront

See map on p70 ←

A DAY IN KUNGSHOLMEN AND VASASTAN

▶ MORNING

Start the day at Stadshuset *(see pp22–3)*: tours start at around 10am and the tower is open from 9:15am from May to September. From Stadshuset take the lovely waterside walk along popular Norr Mälarstrand – perhaps pop into Petite France *(see p74)* for morning coffee and a pastry. Shopping street St Eriksgatan starts at the northeastern corner of Rålambshovsparken and goes right through the main shopping area of Kungsholmen. As well as taking in the shops, including the mall at Fridhemsplan, grab a light lunch at Café Fix, which is at St Eriksgatan 35, and is said to be the oldest café in Stockholm.

AFTERNOON

Crossing St Eriksbron leads to the northern end of St Eriksgatan with its cluster of record stores. From here it is a very short walk to Vasaparken, a lovely park to put your feet up with an ice cream in the summer or try ice-skating in winter. Old-fashioned Konditori Ritorno *(see p74)* is right opposite the park: cozy and warm in the winter and with a sunny outdoor area in the summer. Head on to Odenplan and pop into the Stadsbiblioteket *(see p71)* to admire its impressive rotunda. The Stadsbiblioteket lends more than a million books every year. Round off the day with dinner at Café Tranan *(see p74)* – eat in the restaurant or the bar, before enjoying an after-dinner drink with the local crowd.

Cafés, Bars and Pubs

1 Café Tranan
MAP B1 ■ Karlbergsvägen 14
■ 08 527 281 00 ■ Open 11:30am–
11pm Mon–Fri, noon–11pm Sat–Sun
This basement bar below a
restaurant is the perfect place to
blend in with the locals (see p50).

2 Konditori Ritorno
MAP B2 ■ Odengatan 80–82
■ 08 32 01 06 ■ Open 7am–10pm
Mon–Thu, 7am–8pm Fri, 8am–6pm
Sat, 10am–6pm Sun
Enjoy Swedish filter coffee and
delicious cinnamon buns at this
retro café and patisserie.

3 Konditori Valand
MAP C1 ■ Surbrunnsgatan 48
■ 08 30 04 76 ■ Open 8am–7pm
Mon–Fri, 9am–5pm Sat
This café has remained unchanged
since 1954, with wooden walls and
matching furniture.

4 Vurma
MAP B2 ■ Gästrikegatan 2
■ 08 30 62 30 ■ Open 9am–7pm
Mon–Sat, 10am–7pm Sun
Choose from a great selection of
grilled sandwiches with names such
as "Alien", "Freak" and "Clown".

5 BrewDog Kungsholmen
MAP A2 ■ Sankt Eriksgatan 56
■ 08 650 21 10 ■ Open 4pm–midnight
Mon–Thu, 3pm–1am Fri–Sat
The Scottish craft-beer brand serves
all their hoppy signature brews here
plus select guest pours (see p51).

6 Non Solo Bar
MAP C1 ■ Odengatan 34
■ 08 440 20 82 ■ Open 7am–9pm
Mon–Fri, 9am–6pm Sat–Sun
Highly rated for its coffee, this Italian
café serves classic food such as
pasta, salads and sandwiches.

7 Olssons Skor
MAP C1 ■ Odengatan 41 ■ 08
673 38 00 ■ Open 9pm–3am Wed–Sat
Dark and intimate, this stylish club
plays classic electro beats until late.

8 Petite France
MAP B3 ■ John Ericssonsgatan 6
■ 08 618 28 00 ■ Open 8am–6pm
Mon–Fri, 9am–5pm Sat–Sun
Entering this café feels like stepping
into a traditional French bakery, with
bread and pastries to match.

9 Man in the Moon
MAP C2 ■ Tegnérgatan 2c
■ 08 458 95 00 ■ Open 11am–11pm
Mon, 11am–midnight Tue–Thu,
11am–1am Fri, 2pm–1am Sat
This traditional pub with an English
feel serves different and unusual
types of Swedish beer.

10 Orangeriet
MAP B4 ■ Norr Mälarstrand
Kajplats 464 ■ 08 505 244 75 ■ Open
from 5pm Tue–Thu, 4pm Fri, 1pm Sat
& Sun (no set closing times)
Located on Norr Mälarstrand, this
is a café by day and bar at night.

Bar at BrewDog Kungsholmen

Places to Eat

PRICE CATEGORIES

For a three-course meal for one with half a bottle of wine (or equivalent meal), taxes and extra charges.

Ⓚ under 700 kr   ⒦⒦ 700–1,000 kr
⒦⒦⒦ over 1,000 kr

1 Linguini
MAP B1 ▪ Frejgatan 48 ▪ 08 31 49 15 ▪ Open 5–9pm Mon–Tue, 5–10pm Wed–Fri, 4:30–10pm Sat ▪ Ⓚ Ⓚ
Cozy Linguini serves good Italian food. Book in advance, as there are only around 10 tables.

2 Browallshof
MAP C1 ▪ Surbrunnsgatan 20 ▪ 08 16 51 36 ▪ 5pm–midnight Sat & Mon, 11:30am–midnight Tue–Fri ▪ Ⓚ Ⓚ
Housed in an 18th-century building, this hotel serves classic Swedish dishes, all made with fresh, organic ingredients.

3 Svartengrens
MAP C1 ▪ Tulegatan 24 ▪ 08 612 65 50 ▪ 5pm–1am Tue–Sun ▪ Ⓚ Ⓚ
This restaurant serves ecologically sourced food and good cocktails.

4 Smörgåstårteriet
MAP B2 ▪ Dalagatan 42 ▪ 08 94 91 13 ▪ Open 11:30am–2pm & 5:30pm–11pm Mon–Fri ▪ Ⓚ Ⓚ
This tiny restaurant serves a six-course fixed menu of superb Scandinavian dishes in two sittings.

5 Spisa Hos Helena
MAP B3 ▪ Scheelegatan 18 ▪ 08 654 49 26 ▪ Open 11am–midnight Mon–Fri, 4pm–midnight Sat, 4pm–11pm Sun ▪ Ⓚ
The Sunday set menu offers great value at this cozy and popular bistro.

6 Tennstopet
MAP B2 ▪ Dalagatan 50 ▪ 08 32 25 18 ▪ 11:30am–1am Mon–Fri, 1pm–1am Sat–Sun ▪ Ⓚ Ⓚ
Relive the 1940s and 1950s in this place serving classic Swedish food.

7 Lux Dag för Dag
Primusgatan 116 ▪ 08 619 01 90 ▪ Open 11:30am–2pm & 5–11pm Tue–Fri, 5–11pm Sat ▪ Ⓚ Ⓚ
This Michelin-starred restaurant offers seasonal cooking with locally sourced fresh produce.

Chic interior of Lux Dag för Dag

8 Stadshuskällaren
MAP C4 ▪ Hantverkargatan 1 ▪ 08 586 218 30 ▪ Open 11:30am–2:30pm Mon–Tue, 11:30am–2:30pm and 5–11pm Wed–Fri, 5–11pm Sat ▪ Ⓚ Ⓚ
Sample Nobel Prize banquet menus served since 1901 in the atmospheric vaulted cellar of Stadshuset.

9 Trattorian
MAP B4 ▪ Norr Mälarstrand 9, Kajplats 464 ▪ 08 505 244 50 ▪ Open 5pm–1am Mon–Sat, 5pm–midnight Sun ▪ Ⓚ Ⓚ
Classic Italian cuisine is served on a waterside pontoon, with fabulous views across the water at sunset.

10 Lilla Ego
MAP B1 ▪ Västmannagatan 69 ▪ 08 27 44 55 ▪ Open 5–11pm Tue–Sat ▪ Ⓚ Ⓚ
Enjoy robust, seasonal dishes prepared by award-winning chefs at this warm, friendly restaurant. Book well in advance.

See map on p70 ⟵

TOP 10 Östermalm and Djurgården

Although these two districts are neighbours, Östermalm and Djurgården offer contrasting experiences. Östermalm is the most exclusive part of Stockholm, and is home to some of the city's most expensive restaurants and designer shops. Djurgården, on the other hand, is largely tranquil – it has only 800 permanent residents and is part of the Stockholm National City Park. Most of its eastern end of the island is undisturbed parkland with excellent walks, while the western part is packed with some of Stockholm's top attractions, drawing a multitude of visitors and locals alike – Skansen, Junibacken, Vasamuseet and Gröna Lund funfair are all found here.

Carl Linnaeus statue, Humlegården

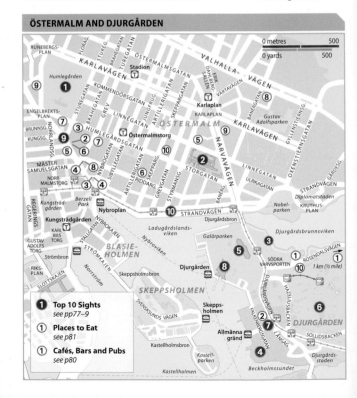

ÖSTERMALM AND DJURGÅRDEN

1	Top 10 Sights	see pp77–9
①	Places to Eat	see p81
①	Cafés, Bars and Pubs	see p80

1 Humlegården
MAP M1

Just a stone's throw away from Stureplan, the broad, oak tree-lined paths and lawns of Humlegården, or "Hop Garden", are a welcome retreat from the busy city centre. This former royal garden has been a public park since 1869, boasting a large play area and, in the summer, outdoor clubs and bars. A statue of Swedish naturalist Carl Linnaeus looks out over the middle of the park. Humlegården is also home to the National Library of Sweden.

2 Historiska Museet

The Swedish History Museum is a showcase for collections from Prehistory through the Viking era to the Middle Ages. Fantastic artifacts include ancient gold jewellery, while a reconstruction shows what a small rural church in Västergötland looked like at the end of the Middle Ages. Discover how people lived, worked and ate during the prehistoric times and view priceless archaeological finds that were discovered after 3,000 years. The Viking exhibitions reveal how these people were often peaceful traders rather than brutal robbers (see pp32–3).

3 Walk along Djurgårdsbrunnsviken
MAP R4

Alight from the bus or tram at Djurgårdsbron, opposite Nordiska Museet. Walk through the bright blue gates to pick up the path along Rosendalsvägen, by the water's

Bridge across Djurgårdsbrunnsviken

edge, and watch gleaming mahogany boats, canoes and pedalos glide past. The path leads towards the biodynamic market garden and café at Rosendals Trädgård (see p80).

4 Gröna Lund

By the Djurgården waterfront, Gröna Lund is both an amusement park and a major concert venue. The funfair features over 30 attractions, including seven roller coasters and one of the world's highest free fall towers. The Eclipse ride is the world's highest StarFlyer at 122m (400 ft). The park also includes vintage carousels and side-shows. There are numerous restaurants, bars and fast food outlets (see pp28–9).

Gröna Lund amusement park

Exhibition hall, Nordiska Museet

5 Nordiska Museet

This lovely museum charts everyday life in Sweden from the 16th century to the present day via a huge number of exhibits. The exhibitions focus on periods of major change and transition – fashion trends are explored from the 1780s, 1860s and 1960s, while a section dedicated to interiors covers both the elaborate styles of the 19th century as well as the practical considerations made for the country's housing boom of the 1970s. Visitors can also find out about how local Swedish traditions such as dancing around the maypole to celebrate Midsummer originated *(see pp30–31)*.

6 Skansen

Located in a beautiful hilly spot on Djurgården, Skansen is deservedly one of the city's most enduring attractions. Journey through Sweden over the ages, or visit Stockholm's only zoo with animals native to Scandinavia such as elk, bears, lynx and wolves. Visit the town district with wooden urban dwellings and crafts such as glass blowing and printing. There is also a terrarium, a monkey house and a zoo for children, as well as gentle fairground rides *(see pp12–13)*.

7 ABBA The Museum

MAP R5 ■ Djurgårdsvägen 68 ■ 08 121 328 60 ■ Opening hours vary, check website for details ■ Adm ■ www.abbathemuseum.com

Fans of the Swedish pop sensation ABBA will love this museum, which features a multitude of interactive displays. Visitors can put on the legendary stage costumes and sing alongside hologram illusions of the band at Polar Studio. The Folkpark exhibition transports visitors to 1966, when the ABBA phenomenon started, as this was where Benny and Björn first met. In addition, listen to the band members' own stories and memories from their amazing award-winning careers *(see p42)*.

8 Vasamuseet

Getting up close to the *Vasa*, the best-preserved 17th-century warship in the world, is a unique and memorable experience. Built as the jewel of the Swedish fleet, she sank just minutes into her maiden voyage from Stockholm in 1628, and lay undisturbed for 333 years. In 1961, an extraordinary salvage operation raised the ship – different exhibitions inside the Vasamuseet describe the story of the vessel and its impressive restoration *(see pp14–15)*.

Bünsowska Huset, Strandvägen

ÖSTERMALM – STOCKHOLM'S EXCLUSIVE DISTRICT

Östermalm was developed in the late 19th century around the four wide, tree-lined boulevards of Karlavägen, Strandvägen, Valhallavägen and Narvavägen. Some of Sweden's best architects of the era shaped the district in a Renaissance style. Östermalm is also home to many embassies and consulates.

9 Stureplan
MAP M2

Originally just the name of a square with a quirky mushroom-shaped rain shelter at its heart, "Stureplan" has become synonymous with luxury and style. On the streets radiating from it are exclusive fashion houses, costly restaurants, bars and clubs.

10 Strandvägen
MAP P3

Completed in time for Stockholm's World Fair in 1897, Strandvägen is one of the most prestigious streets in the city. Running almost parallel to the waterside of Nybroviken, the wide boulevard has an air of old grandeur, enhanced by the vintage trams that rattle along it. Bünsowska Huset, at Nos 29–33, designed by local architects Isak Gustaf Clason and Anders Gustaf Forsberg, sets the standard for the street. The tree-lined middle of the street shades the walking and cycling lanes, while wooden ships line the quays.

A DAY IN ÖSTERMALM AND DJURGÅRDEN

▶ MORNING

Start off, like thousands of people do, at the concrete "mushroom" meeting spot right on **Stureplan**. Directly behind the sculpture is **Sturegallerian** (Stureplan 4), an ideal place to shop for exclusive brands or browse the excellent Hedengrens bookshop, which stocks books in many languages. There are also several cafés to choose from for an energizing morning coffee – the cozy Le Café is recommended. Next, head for the shopping heart of Östermalm in the streets surrounding Östermalmstorg. Drop by the **Östermalms Saluhall**, a 19th-century food hall located on the square, to stock up on some Swedish delicacies. From there, it is a short walk to **Brasserie Elverket** (see p81) on Linnégatan, which is an excellent choice for lunch on weekdays with several good-value dishes of the day.

AFTERNOON

Burn off the calories after lunch by strolling down to **Strandvägen**; either continue along the lovely waterside boulevard admiring the architecture, or hop on to a bus or tram to the parkland island of **Djurgården** (see p45). Alight at **Skansen** (see pp12–13) and set aside an afternoon to wander around its old town, rustic farm houses and Scandinavian zoo. Round off the day with a classic Swedish dinner at **Ulla Windbladh** (see p81). If that is fully booked, the nearby **Villa Godthem** (see p81) is a good second option; both have outdoor seating in summer.

See map on p76 ←

Cafés, Bars and Pubs

1 Rosendals Trädgård
MAP G4 ■ Rosendalsterrassen 12 ■ 08 545 812 70 ■ Open May–Sep: 11am–5pm Mon–Fri, 11am–6pm Sat & Sun; Oct–Apr: 11am–4pm Tue–Sun ■ www.rosendalstradgard.se
This idyllic garden café in Djurgården sells homemade organic salads, soups, sandwiches and pastries.

2 Blå Porten
MAP R5 ■ Djurgårdsvägen 64 ■ 08 663 87 59 ■ Open 11am–9pm Tue–Thu, 11am–7pm Fri–Mon
Close to Gröna Lund, Skansen and Vasamuseet, Blå Porten offers a wide-ranging self-service menu.

Riche, a classic Stockholm bar

3 Riche
MAP N2 ■ Birger Jarlsgatan 4 ■ 08 545 035 60 ■ Open 7:30am–midnight Mon, 7:30am–2am Tue–Fri, noon–2am Sat, noon–midnight Sun
A meeting place with several bars.

4 Sturekatten
MAP N2 ■ Riddargatan 4 ■ 08 611 16 12 ■ Open 9am–7pm Mon–Fri, 10am–6pm Sat, 11am–6pm Sun
The "Sture Cat" is an old-fashioned tea and coffee house in an apartment building from the 1700s.

5 East
MAP M2 ■ Stureplan 13 ■ 08 611 49 59 ■ Open 11:30am–3am Mon–Fri, 5pm–3am Sat & Sun
East serves Asian food by day, and turns into a nightclub after 11pm.

6 Obaren Sturehof
MAP M2 ■ Sturegallerian 42, Stureplan 2 ■ 08 440 57 30 ■ Open 11am–2am Mon–Fri, noon–2am Sat & Sun
Central to Stureplan's busy club scene, Obaren is a good choice for those who just want to party.

7 Scandic Anglais
MAP D2 ■ Humlegårdsgatan 23 ■ 08 517 340 00 ■ Open 9am–midnight Mon–Tue, 9am–2am Wed–Sat, 11am–midnight Sun
With three bars and a summer roof-top terrace, Scandic Anglais has DJs most nights and attracts an after-work and late-night party crowd.

8 Valhallabageriet
MAP R1 ■ Valhallavägen 174 ■ 08 662 97 63 ■ Open 7am–6pm Mon–Fri, 8am–3pm Sat, 9am–3pm Sun
New sourdough bakeries seem to spring up every week in Stockholm, but Valhallabageriet has endured. It also serves good coffee and fabulous Swedish buns and pastries.

9 Saturnus
MAP D2 ■ Eriksbergsgatan 6 ■ 08 611 77 00 ■ Open 8am–8pm Mon–Fri, 9am–7pm Sat & Sun
This Parisian-style café and lunch spot serves big bowls of coffee with cinnamon buns to match. It also serves breakfast and brunch and offers its customers a selection of international newspapers to read.

10 Tudor Arms
MAP P2 ■ Grevgatan 31 ■ 08 660 27 12 ■ Open 11:30am–11pm Mon–Fri, 1–11pm Sat, 1–7pm Sun
British pub the Tudor Arms has been open since 1969.

See map on p76

Places to Eat

PRICE CATEGORIES

For a three-course meal for one with half a bottle of wine (or equivalent meal), taxes and extra charges.

Ⓚ under 700 kr   ⒦⒦ 700–1,000 kr
⒦⒦⒦ over 1,000 kr

1 Villa Godthem
MAP R4 ▪ Rosendalsvägen 9
▪ 08 505 244 15 ▪ Open 11:30am–10pm Mon, 11:30am–11pm Tue–Fri, noon–11pm Sat & Sun ▪ ⒦⒦⒦
Located in a 19th-century wooden house set deep in Djugården parkland, Villa Godthem serves classic gourmet Swedish dishes.

2 Sturehof
MAP M2 ▪ Stureplan 2 ▪ 08 440 57 30 ▪ Open 11am–2am Mon–Fri, noon–2am Sat, noon–2am Sun ▪ ⒦⒦
With a history that spans over a century, this classic restaurant in Östermalm specializes in seafood.

3 Ekstedt
MAP D2 ▪ Humlegårdsgatan 17 ▪ 08 611 12 10 ▪ Open 6pm–1am Tue–Thu, 5pm–1am Fri, 4pm–1am Sat ▪ ⒦⒦⒦
Rustic four- or six-course set menus are cooked on an open, wood fire at superstar chef Niklas Ekstedt's signature Stockholm restaurant.

4 Teatergrillen
MAP N2 ▪ Nybrogatan 3 ▪ 08 545 035 65 ▪ Open Lunch: 11:30am–2pm Mon–Fri; dinner: 5pm–midnight Mon, 5pm–1am Tue–Sat ▪ ⒦⒦
This place is an excellent French-Swedish crossover restaurant.

5 Brasserie Elverket
MAP Q2 ▪ Linnégatan 69 ▪ 08 661 25 62 ▪ Open Lunch: 11am–2pm Mon–Fri; dinner: 5–10pm Mon–Wed; 5–11pm Thu–Sat ▪ ⒦
The lunches at this French-inspired brasserie are superb value and it serves unusual beers on tap.

6 Gastrologik
MAP D3 ▪ Artillerigatan 14
▪ 08 662 30 60 ▪ Open 6–11:30pm Tue–Fri, 5–11:30pm Sat ▪ ⒦⒦⒦
Experience new Nordic cuisine with a tasting menu updated daily to feature the best fresh local produce.

7 Grodan
MAP N2 ▪ Grev Turegatan 16
▪ 08 679 61 00 ▪ Open 7:30am–11pm Mon (to midnight Tue–Thu, to 2am Fri), noon–2am Sat, noon–10pm Sun ▪ ⒦⒦
A classic Swedish-European fusion restaurant with an adjacent bar.

8 PA & Co
MAP N2 ▪ Riddargatan 8
▪ 08 611 08 45 ▪ Open 5pm–midnight daily ▪ ⒦⒦
Swedish food with a twist is served in an intimate space.

9 Cassi
MAP Q2 ▪ Narvavägen 30
▪ 08 661 74 61 ▪ Open 10:45am–8pm Mon–Fri, 1–8pm Sun ▪ ⒦⒦
Go back to the 1970s in this popular family-run French bistro.

10 Ulla Winbladh
MAP R4 ▪ Rosendalsvägen 8
▪ 08 534 897 01 ▪ Open 11:30am–10pm Mon, 11:30am–11pm Tue–Sat, 11:30am–10pm Sun ▪ ⒦⒦
This traditional, historic Swedish inn is located close to Djurgårdsbron.

Alfresco dining at Ulla Winbladh

■TOP10 Gamla Stan, Skeppsholmen and Blasieholmen

The site of Stockholm's 13th-century origins and a well-preserved medieval city centre, Gamla Stan (Old Town) is one of Stockholm's most popular

Lion statue by the Royal Palace

destinations. Away from tourist crowds, however, the narrow streets have a fairy-tale like feel, particularly at night and when it is snowing. The vast and rather sombre-looking Royal Palace is the major attraction, and there are also many beautiful churches, including Storkyrkan. Skeppsholmen is famous for its excellent museums – Moderna Museet, with its collection of 20th-century art, and Östasiatiska Museet, housing Far Eastern antiquities, are two of them. The luxurious Grand Hotel dominates neighbouring Blasieholmen, which is also home to the Nationalmuseum.

GAMLA STAN, SKEPPSHOLMEN AND BLASIEHOLMEN

The small island of Riddarholmen, dominated by Riddarholmskyrkan

1 Riddarholmen
MAP L5 ■ Birger Jarls Torg
■ www.kungahuset.se

The "Knight's Island" is cut off from Gamla Stan by a major road and a river, but is worth the diversion. Usually tranquil, the island has some of the best views in Stockholm from Evert Taubes Terrass across the water to Lake Mälaren. Riddarholmen is home to Riddarholmskyrkan *(see p40)* and many 17th-century palaces, which now house offices. Walpurgis Night *(see p61)* is celebrated here with a bonfire and singing.

2 Nationalmuseum
MAP N4 ■ www.national museum.se

This lavish museum houses Sweden's largest art collection, with some 16,000 paintings and sculptures. There is also a huge collection of drawings and engravings from the Renaissance to the present *(see p43)*.

3 The Royal Palace (Kungliga Slottet)

With more than 600 rooms, the Royal Palace is one of the biggest in Europe and still the venue for all state functions. It houses five museums, including the Treasury, in the cellar vaults, with priceless state regalia such as crowns *(see pp26–7)*.

Gustav III's bedroom, the Royal Palace

4 Storkyrkan
MAP M5 ▪ Trångsund 1
▪ www.svenskakyrkan.se/stockholm
sdomkyrkoforsamling

Stockholm's medieval cathedral, built in 1279, is of great religious importance. It is renowned for its extraordinary art treasures, including *St George and the Dragon* (1489), a sculpture carved from oak and elk horn. The legendary *Vädersolstavlan*, the "Sun Dog Painting", from 1636, is the oldest portrayal of the capital painted from high up on the cliffs of Södermalm. A wide range of services and concerts are held here *(see p40)*.

The red-brick nave of Storkyrkan

5 Stortorget
MAP M5

A small public square, Stortorget, in the middle of Gamla Stan, is the oldest square in Stockholm and the site of the "Stockholm Bloodbath" in 1520 *(see p38)*. Unlike many other European city squares, it was never developed as a showpiece: it has a distinct westward slope, and its buildings were constructed in a haphazard manner in the 17th and 18th centuries. The Stock Exchange Building (Börshuset), in French Rococo style, was completed in 1776 and houses the Nobelmuseet *(see p88)*. In a second-hand shop on Stortorget 5, there are ceiling joists dating from the 1640s with pictures of animals, flowers and fruits.

SLUSSEN REDEVELOPMENT

One of the most historically important junctions in Stockholm is undergoing a controversial transformation. The area around Slussen – the lock between the Baltic and Lake Mälaren, joining Gamla Stan and Södermalm – is being rebuilt to improve traffic flow and to create a new park, plaza and buildings. Building work is expected to last until 2025.

6 Moderna Museet
MAP P4 ▪ Exercisplan 4 ▪ 08 520 235 00 ▪ Open 10am–6pm Tue–Sun (to 8pm Tue) ▪ www.moderna museet.se

Set on the leafy Skeppsholmen island, this museum exhibits key works of 20th-century art, including those by Dalí, Picasso, Matisse, Giorgio de Chirico and many more. The collection includes some 6,000 paintings, sculptures and installations, as well as drawings and photography. The museum also hosts exhibitions of contemporary Swedish and international art. There is a children's workshop, a shop and a restaurant with views across the water to Djurgården and Strandvägen *(see pp42–3)*.

7 Kastellholmen
MAP Q6

South of Skeppsholmen is the tiny island of Kastellholmen, part of the national city park. Take a picnic, find a comfortable spot on its granite rocks, watch the boats go by and admire the Kastellet, the island's castle-like medieval building.

Kastellet on Kastellholmen

The *af Chapman* on Skeppsholmen

8 Skeppsholmen Shoreline Walk
MAP P4

Skeppsholmen is ideal for a circular waterside walk any time of the year. Cross Skeppsholmsbron to the island, turn left and follow the path through a small doorway, and along the water to the quayside Östra Brobänken. Take in the veteran boats moored here, and the views across the water. Catch a Djurgården ferry at the southeastern tip of the island, or continue past the three-mast *af Chapman*, now a hostel *(see p117)*.

9 Christmas Market
MAP M5 ■ Stortorget ■ 4th Sat in Nov–23 Dec: 11am–6pm daily

The magical atmosphere of the Stockholm winter is most evident at the traditional Christmas market in Stortorget. Little red huts sell home-made products – Christmas lights and decorations, handicrafts, festive sweets, smoked sausages, reindeer and elk meat and other delicacies from around Sweden. Get warm with a glass or two of *glögg* (mulled wine).

10 Streets of Gamla Stan
MAP M5

Västerlånggatan is the Old Town's main street, and, although busy, it is no longer as touristy as it used to be. At its southern end is Mårten Trotzigs Gränd, the city's narrowest street. More relaxed Österlånggatan is home to several restaurants and unique shops, and the charming Köpmangatan is a good street to unwind, with the Café Tabac *(see p90)*.

A DAY IN GAMLA STAN, SKEPPSHOLMEN & BLASIEHOLMEN

▶ MORNING

Start the day with a visit to two of Stockholm's best museums: bus 65 from Stockholm's Central Station runs all the way to the island of **Skeppsholmen**. Here, head for the **Moderna Museet**. After a good morning's viewing of its fine 20th-century art collection, take a coffee break at **Café Blom** *(see p90)*, located within the museum. Walk over Skeppsholmsbron towards Blasieholmen and head past the ferries to the **Nationalmuseum** *(see p85)* and the **Grand Hotel** *(see p113)* before swinging back across Strömbron towards the Royal Palace *(see p85)*. Walk up the cobbled Slottsbacken, and on to Gamla Stan's Österlånggatan. A good lunch stop here is **Magnus Ladulås** *(see p91)*; enjoy a three-course meal in their traditional cellar restaurant.

AFTERNOON

Get purposefully lost along the narrow yet charming streets around Köpmangatan, aiming to end up at **Stortorget**, the Old Town's magnificent main square. Admire the square with a hot chocolate at **Chokladkoppen** *(see p90)*. The afternoon can be one of the least busy times on Västerlånggatan; stroll southeast along it and drop into the best of its shops for a leisurely browse. At the eastern end, do not miss the Old Town's narrowest street, Mårten Trotzigs Gränd. Round off the day with a drink and tapas with the locals at popular **Café Tabac** *(see p90)*.

See map on pp84–5 ◀

The Best of the Rest

Models showing changes in historical architectural styles, ArkDes

1 ArkDes
MAP P5 ▪ Exercisplan 4, Skeppsholmen ▪ 08 587 270 00 ▪ Open 10am–8pm Tue, 10am–6pm Wed & Thu, 10am–8pm Fri, 11am–6pm Sat & Sun ▪ Adm ▪ www.arkdes.se

Explore Swedish architecture from 1,000 years ago to the present day.

2 Östasiatiska Museet
MAP P4 ▪ Tyghusplan, Skeppsholmen ▪ 08 519 557 50 ▪ Open 11am–8pm Tue, 11am–5pm Wed–Sun ▪ Adm ▪ www.ostasiatiska.se

This museum has superb collections from the Far East and Asia.

3 Tyska Kyrkan
MAP M5 ▪ Svartmangatan 16 ▪ 08 411 11 88 ▪ Open 1 Oct–30 Apr: noon–4pm Wed, Fri, Sat & Sun; 1 May–30 Sep: noon–4pm daily ▪ www.svenskakyrkan.se/deutschegemeinde

This church was founded in 1571.

4 Story Tours
MAP M5 ▪ 070 490 62 69 ▪ Adm ▪ www.storytours.eu

Discover the Old Town's charms on a walking tour around Gamla Stan.

5 Nobelmuseet
MAP M5 ▪ Stortorget ▪ 08 534 818 00 ▪ Open Jun–Aug: 10am–8pm daily; mid-Sep–May: 11am–8pm Tue, 11am–5pm Wed–Sun ▪ Adm ▪ www.nobelmuseum.se

Learn all about the history of the Nobel Prize and its winners.

6 Livrustkammaren
MAP M5 ▪ Slottsbacken 3 ▪ 08 402 30 30 ▪ Open 11am–5pm daily (to 8pm Thu) ▪ Adm ▪ www.livrustkammaren.se

The Royal Armoury boasts an collection of objects from Swedish royalty.

7 Forum För Levande Historia
MAP M5 ▪ Stora Nygatan 10 ▪ 08 723 87 50 ▪ Open noon–5pm Mon–Fri ▪ www.levandehistoria.se

The Forum for Living History promotes tolerance and human rights.

8 Postmuseum
MAP M5 ▪ Lilla Nygatan 6 ▪ 01 043 644 39 ▪ Open 11am–4pm Tue–Sun; Sep–Apr: till 7pm Wed ▪ Adm ▪ www.postmuseum.posten.se

This museum traces the history of the Swedish postal system.

9 Jarnpojke
MAP E4 ▪ Bollhustäppan

Located just left of the Finska Kyrkan, this 15-cm (5.9-in) statue depicts a boy looking at the moon. Leaving a gift for the statue is said to bring good luck.

10 Fotografins Hus
MAP P4 ▪ Slupskjulsvägen 26c ▪ 08 611 69 69 ▪ Open noon–6pm Wed–Thu, noon–4pm Fri–Sun; closed summers ▪ www.fotografinshus.se

A good collection of contemporary photography is on display here.

Places to Shop

1 Gudrun Sjödén
MAP M5 ▪ Stora Nygatan 33 ▪ 08 23 55 55 ▪ www.gudrunsjoden.com

This place sells colourful clothes for women with an emphasis on Scandinavian style. The garments have been designed by Gudrun Sjödén herself since the 1970s.

2 Iris Hantverk
MAP M5 ▪ Västerlånggatan 24 ▪ 08 698 09 73

Visually impaired craftsmen create "function brushes" at Iris Hantverk, which was established at the end of the 19th century.

Floral dresses, Earth N More

3 Earth N More
MAP M5 ▪ Stora Nygatan 14 ▪ 08 641 02 10

This environmentally conscious store sells clothes and accessories that "combine design, function and environment in an attractive way".

4 Blå Gungan
MAP M5 ▪ Österlånggatan 16, 08 20 23 73 ▪ Open 11am–6pm Mon–Fri, 11am–4pm Sat ▪ www.bla gungan.se

Quirky interior design pieces, accessories, garments and more by mainly Swedish designers.

5 BluVelvet
MAP M5 ▪ Västerlånggatan 32 ▪ 08 10 58 28

A huge selection of fun and trendy clothes, bags and accessories mainly for teens and women in their 20s is available here, though all lovers of funky items are welcome.

6 Happy Sthlm
MAP M5 ▪ Stora Nygatan 36 ▪ 08 642 15 05 ▪ Open 11am–6pm Mon–Fri, 11am–4pm Sat ▪ www. happysthlm.se

Minimalist, functional and attractive handmade fabrics, textiles, ceramics, and jewellery by Swedish designers Katarina Andersson, Kajsa Aronsson and Caroline Lindholm are sold here.

7 Krabat
MAP M5 ▪ Stora Nygatan 21 ▪ 08 21 49 24 ▪ Open 10am–6pm Mon–Fri, 10am–4pm Sat, 11am–4pm Sun ▪ www.krabat.se

The classic and durable toys in the shop's own design are sold next to international brands. Items range from dolls and cars to costumes.

8 SF Bokhandeln
MAP M5 ▪ Västerlånggatan 48 ▪ 08 21 50 52

A haven for lovers of science fiction, this store sells books, films, games and magazines. A large amount of its stock is in English.

9 Edblad
MAP M5 ▪ Västerlånggatan 36 ▪ 08 519 90 092 ▪ Open 10am–6pm Mon–Fri, 10am–5pm Sat, 11am–4pm Sun ▪ www.edblad.com

Designers Hans and Cathrine Edblad create jewellery, clothing and home furnishings made with sustainability in mind. Everything is made in their studio on Singö island.

10 Made In Stockholm
MAP M5 ▪ Västerlånggatan 58 ▪ 08 411 46 07 ▪ Open 11am–6pm Mon–Fri, 11am–4pm Sat & Sun ▪ www.madeinstockholm.nu

Glassware, ceramics, silverware and other handcrafted items are stocked here, made by local artisan designers working in-store.

See map on pp84–5 ←

Cafés, Bars and Pubs

① Café Tabac
MAP M5 ■ Stora Nygatan 46 ■ 08 10 15 34 ■ Open 10am–midnight Mon–Thu, 10am–1am Fri–Sat, 11am–midnight Sun

Popular with the locals, Tabac serves coffee, tapas or a full meal.

② Wirströms Pub
MAP M5 ■ Stora Nygatan 13 ■ 08 21 28 74 ■ Open 11am–1am Mon–Sat, noon–midnight Sun

This popular pub attracts a mix of students, tourists and locals.

③ Stampen
MAP M5 ■ Stora Nygatan 5 ■ 08 20 57 93 ■ Open 5pm–1am Mon–Thu, 8pm–2am Fri–Sat, 1–5pm on some Sun

Founded in 1968, this long-standing jazz and blues bar has live music.

④ Ardbeg Embassy
MAP M5 ■ Västerlånggatan 68 ■ 08 791 90 90 ■ Open 4–10pm Mon–Tue, 4–11pm Wed–Thu, 11am–midnight Fri, noon–midnight Sat

A specialist whisky bar with a wide selection of beers from Swedish micro-breweries. It serves high-quality, pricey food, too.

⑤ Monks Porter House
MAP M5 ■ Munkbron 11 ■ 08 23 12 12 ■ Open from 5pm Tue–Thu, from 4pm Fri & Sat; closes at 1am, or earlier if not busy

Sister pub to the popular Monks Café and Brewery (see p68), Monks Porter House has 56 different beers on tap.

Swanky Cadier Bar in the Grand Hotel

⑥ Lydmar Hotel Bar
MAP N4 ■ Södra Blasieholmshamnen 2 ■ 08 22 31 60 ■ Open 11am–1am daily ■ www.lydmar.com

Great drinks are served in this stylish bar located in the Lydmar Hotel.

⑦ Pubologi
MAP M5 ■ Stora Nygatan 20 ■ 08 506 400 86 ■ Open 5:30–11pm Mon–Sat; closed summer ■ www.pubologi.se

This sleek gastropub has an eclectic menu of pub and bar-style food.

⑧ Chokladkoppen
MAP M5 ■ Stortorget 18 ■ 08 20 31 70 ■ Summer: open 9am–11pm daily; winter: open 10am–10pm Mon–Thu, 10am–11pm Fri, 9am–11pm Sat, 9am–10pm Sun

A gay-friendly café in the Old Town's main square. As the name suggests, there's hot chocolate in abundance.

⑨ Café Blom
MAP P4 ■ Skeppsholmen 7 ■ 08 519 562 91 ■ Open 11am–7:30pm Tue & Fri, 11am–5:30pm Wed, Thu, Sat & Sun

Located close to Moderna Museet and ArkDes, this café serves snacks and pastries. It also has a covered outdoor area in Picasso Park.

⑩ Cadier Bar, Grand Hotel
MAP N4 ■ Södra Blasieholmshamnen 8 ■ 08 679 35 00 ■ Open 7am–2am Mon–Fri, 8am–2am Sat, 8am–1am Sun

Enjoy a glass of wine or a cocktail at the Grand Hotel's elegant bar.

Places to Eat

PRICE CATEGORIES

For a three-course meal for one with half a bottle of wine (or equivalent meal), taxes and extra charges.

Ⓚ under 700 kr   ⓀⓀ 700–1,000 kr
ⓀⓀⓀ over 1,000 kr

1 Restaurang le Rouge
MAP N5 ■ Brunnsgränd 2
■ 08 505 244 30 ■ Open 6pm–1am
Tue–Fri, 5pm–1am Sat ■ ⓀⓀ
Classy but cool French-themed restaurant with opulent interiors.

2 Mathias Dahlgren
MAP N4 ■ Södra
Blaiseholmshamnen 6 ■ 08 679 35 00
■ Open 7pm–midnight Tue–Sat
■ www.grandhotel.se ■ ⓀⓀⓀ
Food in the Grand Hotel's restaurant is made by one of Sweden's top chefs.

3 B.A.R.
MAP N3 ■ Blasieholmsgatan 4a
■ 08 611 53 35 ■ Open 10–1am Mon–Fri, 4pm–1am Sat, 5–9pm Sun ■ ⓀⓀ
Excellent seafood restaurant; pick from grilled fish of the day.

4 The Flying Elk
MAP D4 ■ Mälartorget 15
■ 08 20 85 83 ■ Open 5pm–midnight Mon–Tue, 5pm–1am Wed–Fri, noon–1am Sat, noon–midnight Sun ■ Ⓚ
Swedish culinary tradition meets British pub culture at Swede Björn Frantzén's gastropub.

5 Bistro Pastis
MAP M5 ■ Baggensgatan 12
■ 08 20 20 18 ■ Lunch: Open 11:30am– 3pm Mon–Fri; Dinner: from 5pm Mon–Sat ■ ⓀⓀ
This is an authentic French bistro with a homely, modern feel.

6 Djuret
MAP M5 ■ Lilla Nygatan 5 ■ 08 506 400 84 ■ Open 5:30pm–midnight Mon–Sat ■ ⓀⓀ
With its name meaning "The Animal", Djuret is a meat-eater's paradise.

7 Hotel Skeppsholmen Restaurant
MAP P5 ■ Gröna Gången 1 ■ 08 407 23 05 ■ Open 11:30am–9pm Mon–Fri, noon–9pm Sat & Sun ■ ⓀⓀ
Modern Swedish cuisine is served at this hotel's *(see p114)* restaurant.

Hotel Skeppsholmen Restaurant

8 Omakase Köttslöjd
MAP D4 ■ Yxsmedsgränd 12
■ 08 506 400 80 ■ Open 5pm–11pm Tue–Sat ■ ⓀⓀⓀ
Expect high-end Japanese tasting menus made from produce supplied by their own dedicated butcher.

9 Den Gyldene Freden
MAP N5 ■ Österlånggatan 51 ■ 08 24 97 60 ■ Open 11:30am–2:30pm & 5–10pm Mon–Fri (to 11pm Fri), 1–11pm Sat ■ ⓀⓀ
Owned by the Swedish Academy, this old-fashioned, classic restaurant opened in 1722.

10 Magnus Ladulås
MAP N5 ■ Österlånggatan 26
■ 08 21 19 57 ■ Open 11am–10pm Mon–Thu, 11am–11pm Fri, 1–11pm Sat ■ ⓀⓀ
The three-course meal offers in this cozy cellar restaurant in the heart of the Old Town are particularly good.

See map on pp84–5

TOP 10 Södermalm

Formerly a rough working-class district, Södermalm has been transformed over the last few decades, blossoming into the area to see and in which to be seen. From the hip SoFo district in the east to Hornstull at the island's western tip, which has come up considerably in recent years, "Söder" offers a blend of not-too-pricey restaurants, cool cafés, trendy shopping and a vibrant nightlife. The area has lots of greenery, and some of the best views over Stockholm – particularly from Monteliusvägen, looking across Lake Mälaren to Stadshuset. There is no shortage of museums either, notably the Fotografiska, which has earned immense international acclaim.

Tek (Play) (1935) by Bror Hjorth in Nytorget, SoFo

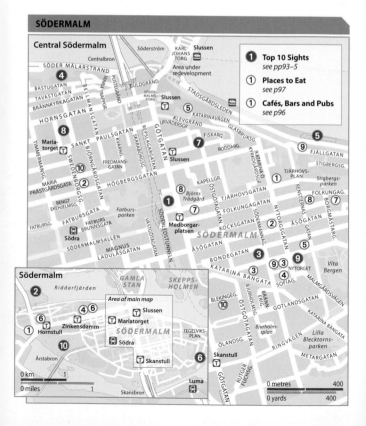

SÖDERMALM

Top 10 Sights *see pp93–5*

Places to Eat *see p97*

Cafés, Bars and Pubs *see p96*

Bustling Medborgarplatsen

1 Medborgarplatsen
MAP D5

"Citizen Square" lives up to its name with a host of communal activities in and around it. In summer it comes alive with a row of outdoor bars and restaurants; in winter there is an ice-skating rink. It is also a gathering place for protests and the starting point for the May Day Parade *(see p61)*. The square is bordered by the Saluhall shopping and entertainment centre, which includes bars, good restaurants and a cinema.

2 Långholmen
MAP A4

This hilly island is a local favourite for walking, picnics, swimming and recreation. Yet from 1880 to 1975, it was home to the country's biggest prison, and Sweden's last execution took place here in 1910. The prison has been converted into a hotel and

Canoeing off Långholmen

youth hostel *(see p117)*. The island has beaches and open-air stages, and is also home to Mälarvarvet, one of Stockholm's oldest shipyards.

3 SoFo
MAP D6 ■ www.sofo-stockholm.se

Short for "South of Folkungagatan", the name is a nod to the Soho districts of London and New York. The quarter is densely packed with cool, quirky and interesting shops specializing in everything from clothing and design to jewellery, vintage, homeware, music and much more. There is also a thriving restaurant and bar scene here. The last Thursday of every month is SoFo Night, when many retailers are open late and often offer special deals.

4 Monteliusvägen
MAP L6

This 500-m-(1,640-ft)-long walking path adjacent to popular Ivar Los Park offers magnificent views of Lake Mälaren, Stadshuset, Gamla Stan and Riddarholmen, especially at sunrise and sunset. Constructed in 1998 on a precipice, it has charming old houses on one side and wonderful views on the other as well as benches and picnic tables from which to enjoy them. However, the path has areas of clay and wooden planks that can be very slippery in winter. On Blecktornsgränd, leading down to Mariatorget towards the eastern end of the walk, there are several cafés.

STIEG LARSSON'S STOCKHOLM

Södermalm became famous with the popularity of author Stieg Larsson's Millennium trilogy – particularly since the Hollywood version of *The Girl With the Dragon Tattoo* was partly filmed on Söder. The Stockholm City Museum offers "Millennium walks", and locations include Mellqvist's Kaffebar, where Larsson himself used to hang out.

5 Fotografiska

MAP E5 ■ Stadsgårdshamnen 22 ■ 08 509 005 00 ■ www.foto grafiska.eu

Billed as a centre for contemporary photography, Fotografiska was opened in 2010 to host works by famous exponents of that art. The brick building from 1906 at the waterfront that houses it was formerly a customs house – it now includes a bistro, café and bar.

The brick exterior of Fotografiska

6 Spårvägsmuseet

MAP F6 ■ Tegelsviksgatan 22 ■ 08 686 17 60 ■ Closed until 2019 ■ Adm ■ www.sparvagsmuseet.sl.se

While this transport museum begins with the horse and cart and simple ferry boats, the main focus is the expansion of the public transport network in the 20th century. Visitors climb aboard trams and buses to be whisked back in time: films projected through tram windows re-create travelling in Stockholm in the 1950s and 1960s. Children can ride aboard a mini-train.

Mosebacke Torg on a summer's day

7 Mosebacke and Mosebacke Torg

MAP D5

The district of Mosebacke has become a cultural centre thanks to Södra Teatern, which hosts music and threatrical events, and its bar. When the weather turns milder, the large open-air section of Södra Bar becomes crowded every evening. Mosebacke Torg, the square, is more peaceful – an oasis with a summer café selling cinnamon buns.

8 Mariatorget

MAP C5

A pretty, quiet square with a gently splashing fountain, Mariatorget is a popular meeting place year round and attracts plenty of sunbathers in summer. It is the perfect spot to rest tired feet. St Paulskyrkan, a small 1876 Methodist church, faces the southwest corner of the square. Mariatorget and the streets around it, St Paulsgatan, Krukmarkargatan and Swedenborgsgatan, are popular with locals for shopping and dining.

9 Skånegatan

MAP D6

The focal point of SoFo, Skånegatan is one of the city's hippest streets with designer shops and alternative bars such as Snotty Sounds Bar and Pet Sounds Bar *(see p96)*. Families fill the area around Nytorget square during the day, and it is not far to

Monteliusvägen | Gondolen | Fotografiska
Maria Magdalena Kyrka
Mellqvist Kaffebar | Mosebacke | SoFo
Katarina Kyrka
Swedish Hasbeens
Pet Sounds Bar
Snotty Sounds Bar | Nytorget Urban Deli

▶ MORNING

Start the day with a cup of coffee or breakfast at **Mellqvist Kaffebar** *(see p96)* then take the short walk up Torkel Knutsonssgatan to the scenic walk along **Monteliusvägen** *(see p93)* towards Slussen. After enjoying the views across Lake Mälaren, descend to 18th-century **Maria Magdalena Kyrka** *(see p41)*. Rising like a crane over Slussen is an old "lift" (no longer in use), on top of which is **Gondolen** *(see p97)*, which is quite a unique place to eat and has a good value lunchtime menu.

AFTERNOON

From Gondolen it is just a short walk to the picturesque square at **Mosebacke**. Enjoy a short, peaceful walk around the square until you reach Östgötagatan; follow it down the hill, perhaps taking a short diversion down Högbergsgatan to **Katarina Kyrka** *(see p41)* and see its attractive grounds. Cross Folkungagatan and reach the heart of **SoFo** *(see p93)*. After browsing the many design shops in the area, such as **Swedish Hasbeens** *(see p56)*, walk north-east along along Renstiernas gata, down the Söderbergs stairs to the waterfront **Fotografiska museum** *(see p94)* on Stadsgårdshamnen. Housed in the former customs house, the museum has cutting-edge international exhibits and a buzzing cafe. Return to Skånegatan for dinner at **Nytorget Urban Deli** *(see p97)* and maybe even an after-dinner drink at **Snotty Sounds Bar** or **Pet Sounds Bar** *(see p96)*.

Vitabergsparken, which stages some free open-air music and dance events during the summer. Bars and restaurants in the area are lively at night, even on weekdays.

🔟 Tantolunden
MAP B6

People meet for swimming and picnics in this large park by the waters of Årstaviken bay in summer – it can get a bit busy on sunny weekends – and for sledding in winter. There is a playground, a beach volleyball court and golf, plus cafés. The park is often used as a festival area, notably for the annual Stockholm Pride festival *(see p60)*. Move away from the crowds and wander up the hill amidst more than 100 allotment gardens and cottages. The Zinkensdamm hotel and hostel *(see p117)* is in the park.

A quiet corner of Tantolunden

See map on p92 ←

Cafés, Bars and Pubs

1 Greasy Spoon
MAP E5 ■ Tjärhovsgatan 19
■ 72 264 20 97 ■ Open 8am–4pm
Mon–Fri, 9am–5pm Sat–Sun ■ www.
greasyspoon.se

Leading the British invasion on
Södermalm, this popular brunch
café is the place to go for a full
English, eggs Benedict or the like.

**2 Morfar Ginko and
Pappa Ray Ray**
MAP C5 ■ Swedenborgsgatan 13
■ 08 641 13 40

Sit outside on the street front or in
the cozy courtyard in summer. It
serves both snacks and full meals.

3 Pet Sounds Bar
MAP D6 ■ Skånegatan 80
■ 08 643 82 25 ■ Open 5pm–midnight
Tue, 5pm–1am Wed–Sat

Named after The Beach Boys' "Pet
Sounds" album and the record store
across the road of the same name,
this place takes its music seriously.
DJs play both in the upstairs bar and
in the cellar at weekends. It has a
good beer selection.

4 Häktet
MAP C5 ■ Hornsgatan 82 ■ 08
84 59 10 ■ Open 5pm–1am Mon–Wed,
5pm–3am Thu–Sat ■ www.haktet.se

A former prison turned popular
late-night haunt serving good food,
beer, wine and cocktails (see p51).

5 Bar Central
MAP E6 ■ Skånegatan 83 ■
08 644 24 20 ■ Open 5pm–midnight
Tue–Fri, 1pm–midnight Sat, 1–10pm
Sun ■ www.barcentral.se

This bar does good, hearty Central
European food, beers and wines in
stylish retro-minimal surrounds.

6 Mellqvist Kaffebar
MAP C5 ■ Hornsgatan 78
■ 07 687 529 92 ■ Open 7am–6pm
Mon–Fri, 9am–6pm Sat & Sun

Renowned for its coffee, Mellqvist
Kaffebar also has a good breakfast.

Old-fashioned bar at Kvarnen

7 Kvarnen
MAP D5 ■ Tjärhovsgatan 4
■ 08 643 03 80 ■ Open 11am–1am
Mon–Tue, 11am–3am Wed–Sat,
noon–11pm Sun

An old-fashioned Swedish beer hall,
Kvarnen becomes a popular bar-
nightclub on weekends (see p50).

8 Babylon
MAP D5 ■ Björns
Trädgårdsgränd ■ 08 640 80 83
■ Open 11am–midnight daily

Hidden in a park just across the road
from bustling Medborgarplatsen,
Babylon has a long, narrow bar that
is perfect for almost any occasion at
any time of the day or year.

9 Snotty Sounds Bar
MAP D6 ■ Skånegatan 90 ■ 08
644 39 10 ■ Open 4pm–1am daily

Probably the only "hole in the wall"
music bar in the city, Snotty has pictures of new wave and punk icons on
the walls and plays tunes to match.
It is small and can get very crowded
at weekends (see p50).

10 Johan and Nyström
MAP C5 ■ Hamringevägen 1
■ 08 530 22 440 ■ Open 7am–8pm
Mon–Fri, 8am–7pm Sat, 9am–6pm
Sun ■ www.johanochnystrom.se

The concept store of these specialist
coffee roasters is a must visit for
anyone serious about the black stuff.

See map on p92

Places to Eat

1 Calexico's
MAP A5 ▪ Hornstulls Strand 4
▪ 08 658 63 50 ▪ Open 5pm–11pm
Tue–Thu, 5pm–1am Fri–Sat,
11am–4pm Sun ▪ Ⓚ
Excellent organic Cal-Mex cuisine
and great cocktails are served here.

2 Meatballs for the People
MAP D5 ▪ Nytorgsgatan 30 ▪ 08
466 60 99 ▪ Open 11am–10pm Sun–
Thu, 11am–midnight Fri–Sat ▪ ⓀⓀ
The classic Swedish dish is done
14 different ways at this trendy spot.

3 Nytorget Urban Deli
MAP E6 ▪ Nytorget 4 ▪ 08 599
091 80 ▪ Open 8am–11pm Sun–Tue,
8am–midnight Wed–Thu, 8am–1am
Fri–Sat ▪ ⓀⓀ
A restaurant, bar and food store with
a lively New York feel (see p54).

4 Vina
MAP E6 ▪ Sofiagatan 1 ▪ 70
406 66 26 ▪ Open 4–10pm Tue–Thu,
4–11pm Fri, 1–11pm Sat ▪ Ⓚ
This restaurant serves tapas, seasonal
dishes and excellent natural wines.

5 Gondolen
MAP D5 ▪ Stadsgården 6 ▪ 08
641 70 90 ▪ Open Lunch: 11:30am–
2:30pm Tue–Fri; Dinner: 5–11pm Mon,
5pm–1am Tue–Fri, 4pm–1am Sat ▪ ⓀⓀ
Fine-dining atop Katarinahissen,
a Stockholm landmark.

6 Linje Tio
MAP A5 ▪ Hornsbruksgatan 24
▪ 08 22 00 21 ▪ Open 5pm–1am Mon–
Thu, 4pm–2am Fri, noon–2am Sat,
noon–1am Sun ▪ Ⓚ
Continental European cocktail bar
and restaurant, popular with the
after-work crowd for refreshers or
late nights out in the increasingly
fashionable Hornstull area.

7 Punk Royale
MAP E5 ▪ Folkungagatan 128
▪ 08 31 13 33 13 ▪ Open 6pm–
midnight Tue–Fri ▪ ⓀⓀⓀ
A young maverick on the Stockholm
dining scene, Punk Royale tears up
the rule book with edgy dishes in a
high-energy environment (see p55).

8 Deli Di Luca
MAP E5 ▪ Folkungagatan 110
▪ 08 644 04 20 ▪ Open 7:30am–10pm
Mon–Wed, 7:30am–11pm Thu–Fri,
10am–11pm Sat ▪ ⓀⓀ
A taste of Italy with a Nordic twist.
Sit in for a meal or buy ingredients
to take away for a picnic.

9 Hermans
MAP E5 ▪ Fjällgatan 23b ▪ 08
643 94 80 ▪ Open 11am–10pm daily
▪ Ⓚ
With an all-you-can-eat vegetarian
buffet, Hermans offers great variety.

10 Pelikan
MAP D6 ▪ Blekingegatan 40
▪ 08 556 090 90 ▪ Open 5pm–
midnight Mon–Thu, 1pm–1am Fri &
Sat, 1–11pm Sun ▪ ⓀⓀ
Enjoy traditional Swedish food in a
17th-century beer hall setting.

Traditional interior of Pelikan

TOP 10 Further Afield

It is easy to venture beyond Stockholm – and there is plenty to see. SL Access cards (see p101) are great value for those who want to roam as the Greater Stockholm travel card zone extends to the port of Nynäshamn in the south and beyond Norrtälje in the north. Buses usually run to the most out-of-the-way sights, even the wilderness of Tyresö National Park. The city of Uppsala is one of the best day trips from the city, as is the Stockholm Archipelago.

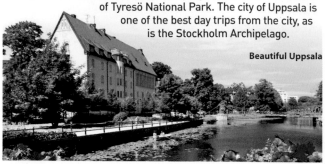

Beautiful Uppsala

FURTHER AFIELD

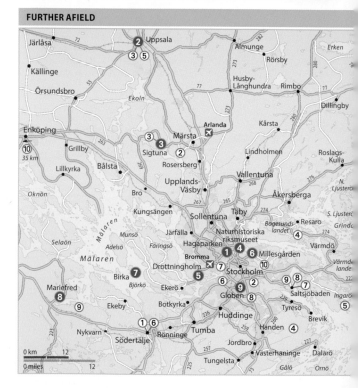

1 Hagaparken

This "English Park" has softly shaped lawns interspersed with dark forests where paths meander amidst elegant trees, and with pavilions and ruins offering constant surprises. It lies just north of the city and is easily reached by bus (see pp34–5).

2 Uppsala

Sweden's fourth-biggest city and a major university town founded in 1477, Uppsala is picturesque and lively, with a striking cathedral. SL commuter trains take under an hour from Stockholm to Uppsala station, right in the city centre.

3 Sigtuna

Founded in 980, Sigtuna is Sweden's oldest city. It has a very popular centre, with low wooden houses, lots of cafés, craft shops and

Ruins of St Olof's church, Sigtuna

a charming museum. There are also the ruins of two churches – St Olof's and St Per's. The city can be easily reached by local train to Märsta followed by a short connecting bus ride. Boat trips to Sigtuna operate from Stockholm during the summer, travelling through Lake Mälaren.

4 Naturhistoriska Riksmuseet

MAP C1 ■ Frescativägen 40 ■ 08 519 540 40 ■ Adm ■ www.nrm.se

The natural sciences are presented in a lively and interactive manner at this natural history museum. Varied exhibits showcase everything from the history of life and the origin of species to visits to polar regions and the treasures of the earth's interior. Adventures with dinosaurs and in outer space come to life at the IMAX cinema, Cosmonova (see p49).

Naturhistoriska Riksmuseet exhibit

Arholma

Röksta · Harg

Norrtälje

Gisslingö

Kapellskär

Gråskö

Hysingsvik

Yxlan Blidö

Lagnö

①

Stockholm Möja
archipelago
⑩ Möja

·indö

Djurö
Stavsnäs

Sandön

Runmarö
·gelbrolandet

Baltic
Sea

Nämndö

CARL MILLES

Known as Sweden's most famous sculptor, Carl Milles (1875–1955) was an assistant to French sculptor Auguste Rodin in Paris and spent over 20 years in the United States – many major municipal buildings in America include his sculptures. Milles and his wife Olga acquired the house at Millesgården in 1906, and its spacious terraces were developed over the next 50 years.

Drottningholm palace and gardens

5 Drottningholm

One of the best day trips from Stockholm, Drottningholm's Royal Palace and its park is one of three UNESCO World Heritage sites in and around the city (see pp24–5).

6 Millesgården

Herserudsvägen 32, Lidingö ▪ www. millesgarden.se

This spectacular park overlooking the water includes sculptor Carl Milles's most famous works arranged on terraces below his former home. In 1936, Carl and his wife Olga donated Millesgården to the Swedes; castings of some of his sculptures are still sold in very limited editions to help fund the property's upkeep. Millesgården is an easy and pleasant trip from Stockholm; take the tram from Ropsten.

Viking coin, Birka

7 Birka

A UNESCO World Heritage Site, Birka is one of the most complete examples of a Viking trading settlement from around the 8th and 9th centuries. While practically nothing remains above ground of what existed during that era, a museum illustrates how the town looked and functioned, and there are some remarkable finds here. The island itself is calm and unspoilt with sheep and bull calves roaming about. Birka can be reached by boat trips in the summer.

8 Mariefred

Dominated by the fairytale-like Gripsholm Castle, the charming town of Mariefred is characterized by narrow streets and low wooden buildings in soft colours, mostly dating from the 18th and 19th centuries. It is a popular day trip; in summer take the steamboat, S/S *Mariefred*, from Stadshuskajen, next to Stadshuset. It is also possible to take a train from Stockholm to Läggesta and change to the Östra Södermalms steam railway to Mariefred (summer only). Combine the trip here with a visit to the Taxinge Slott (see p102).

Gripsholm Castle, Mariefred

9 Ericsson Globen

Globentorget 2 ■ 07 718 110 00
■ Open 9am–6pm Mon–Fri, 9:30am–
4pm Sat & Sun; extended opening
hours in summer ■ Adm: Skyview
■ www.globearenas.se

Not only is Globen (see p47) an
excellent indoor arena for sport
and concerts, but also the largest
spherical building in the world. The
white ball can be seen for miles
around – and it is possible to travel
to the top and enjoy great views
through the glass gondolas running
on tracks fixed to the globe's exterior.
The trip is always a popular one –
even weddings take place in the
gondolas – so book ahead.

Rödlöga, Stockholm Archipelago

10 Stockholm Archipelago

One could spend a few weeks
exploring Stockholm's wonderful
archipelago, but it is still possible to
sample many of its delights even on
a short trip. The main town on the
archipelago is picturesque Vaxholm,
with its well-preserved wooden
houses dating from the turn of the
nineteenth century, painted in delicate
pastel tones. There are charming
harbour-side restaurants and cafés,
and it is easily accessible year round,
by Waxholmsbolagets boat or by bus
670 from Stockholm (see pp16–17).

DAY TRIP TO UPPSALA

Linnéträdgården (Linnaeus Garden)

Linnémuseet
(Linnaeus Museum)

Lannakatten
Narrow Gauge
Railway

Uppsala
Central

Uppsala
Cathedral   Hambergs Fisk

Marielund
(16 km)

▶ MORNING

Uppsala (see p99) is perfect for
a day trip, with most of its sights
concentrated in the historic western side of the city. The centre of
town is within easy walking dis-
tance from the central railway
station. On arrival, turn right out
of the station; it is a short walk
to the north to the beautifully
laid-out Linnaeus Garden and
Museum and Botanical Gardens.
Cross the river and swing back
along its course to the Uppsala
Cathedral, dating back to the
13th century and the tallest
church building in Scandinavia.
King Gustav Vasa is buried here.
Hambergs Fisk (see p103) is just
a stone's throw from the cathedral, and as one of the best-rated
restaurants in the city, an ideal
stop for lunch. Its lunch menu
offers excellent value compared
to the evening à la carte dishes.

AFTERNOON

On the eastern side of Uppsala
station is the terminus of the
**Lennakatten Narrow Gauge
Railway** (see p102). The 32-km
(20-mile) route wends through
forests and past lakes, with
six different station stops: for a
return trip to Marielund allow
around two hours, which will
give ample time for a stroll and
refreshments in the station café.
From Uppsala there are regular
trains for Stockholm (around
three direct trains per hour until
late evening). If you are staying
here for dinner, the last direct
train to Stockholm from Uppsala
station departs at around 10pm.

See map on pp98–9

The Best of the Rest

1 Torekällberget Outdoor Museum, Södertälje
Torekällberget,151 89 Södertälje ▪ 08 523 014 22 ▪ Open 1 Sep–31 May: 10am–4pm daily; 1 Jun–31 Aug: 10am–5pm daily

The museum houses a quaint village, exhibitions and animals that were once common on local farms.

2 Steninge Slott
Steninge Slottsväg 141, 195 91 Märsta ▪ Train from Stockholm to Märsta, then bus 580 and walk 2 km (1 mile) ▪ 08 592 595 00 ▪ Open 11am–6pm Mon–Fri, 10am–5pm Sat & Sun

This Baroque palace is located by the waters of Lake Mälaren near Märsta. It hosts a Christmas market.

3 Lennakatten Narrow Gauge Railway, Uppsala
Uppsala Östra station, Uppsala ▪ 01 813 05 00 ▪ Open from early Jun–early Sep ▪ Adm

Ride this steam train from Uppsala through dense forests and lakes.

Tyresta National Park at dawn

4 Tyresta National Park
Tyresta village, 136 59 Vendelsö ▪ 08 745 33 94 ▪ Buses 807 & 809

Just 20 km (12 miles) from central Stockholm, this is a vast area of unspoilt beauty, superb for hiking.

5 Björnö
MAP H2 ▪ Buses 428 & 429

Located on Ingarö island, this nature reserve has beaches and camping.

The sprawling Tom Tits Experiment

6 Tom Tits Experiment, Södertälje
Storgatan 33, 151 36 Södertälje ▪ 08 550 225 00 ▪ Open 10am–5pm Mon–Tue & Fri, 10am–7pm Thu, 10am–6pm Sat & Sun ▪ Adm

Spend at least half a day in this interactive science museum, which has attractions for all ages.

7 Saltsjöbaden
Take the Saltsjöbanan light train to this beautiful seaside resort. An organic café, Stationhuset, sells lunches and snacks year round.

8 Skogskyrkogården
Skogskyrkogården ▪ 08 508 317 30

Actress Greta Garbo is buried in this cemetery, which is a UNESCO World Heritage Site.

9 Taxinge Slott
Taxinge Slott, Taxinge ▪ 01 597 01 14 ▪ www.taxingeslott.se

This castle is famous for its cake buffet featuring an impressive 65 types of locally baked cakes.

10 Västerås
One of Sweden's oldest cities, Västerås has many museums, shops, a cathedral and a botanic garden.

See map on pp98–9

Cafés and Restaurants

① Finnhamns Café & Krog
Finnhamns brygga ▪ 08 542 464 04 ▪ Open Jun–Aug: 11am–midnight daily; May, Sep–Oct: 11am–midnight Sat & Sun ▪ (Kr)

Enjoy a glass of wine and sumptuous dishes while taking in the great views.

② Nya Carnegiebryggeriet
Ljusslingan 15–17 ▪ 08 510 650 82 ▪ Open 4pm–midnight Tue–Sat ▪ www.nyacarnegiebryggeriet.se ▪ (Kr)(Kr)

A must-visit for craft-beer lovers, this is a brewery, bar and restaurant in the Hammarby Sjöstad district.

③ Båthuset
Hamnen, Sigtuna ▪ 08 592 567 80 ▪ Open May–Sep: 6–10pm Tue–Sat; Oct–Apr: 6–9pm Wed–Sat ▪ (Kr)

This floating restaurant exudes quality and has a homely ambience.

④ Vaxholms Hembygdsgårds Café
Trädgårdsgatan 19, Vaxholm ▪ 08 541 319 80 ▪ Open weekends in May, daily Jun–mid-Sep ▪ (Kr)

A pretty waterfront café serving light Swedish food such as salads, waffles, pancakes and open sandwiches.

⑤ Hambergs Fisk
Fyristorg 8, Uppsala ▪ 01 871 21 50 ▪ Open 11:30am–10pm Tue–Sat ▪ (Kr)(Kr)

This small seafood restaurant has a French bistro-like atmosphere.

⑥ Landet
LM Ericssons väg 27, Telefonplan ▪ 08 410 193 20 ▪ Open 5pm–midnight Mon–Thu, 5pm–1am Fri–Sat ▪ (Kr)

Trendy Landet is a restaurant, bar, club and live music venue in one.

⑦ Sjöpaviljongen
Traneberg Strand 4, Bromma ▪ 08 704 04 24 ▪ Open 11:15am–10pm Mon–Fri, noon–10pm Sat, noon–9pm Sun ▪ (Kr)(Kr)

Set in lovely waterside surroundings, Sjöpaviljongen has a terrace to eat on in the summer.

⑧ Stationshuset i Saltsjöbaden
Saltsjöbaden station ▪ 08 556 266 00 ▪ Open 9am–5pm daily ▪ (Kr)

Organic food is served in this former station house, where trains heading here from Slussen terminate.

⑨ Skärgårdskrogen i Saltsjöbaden
Vikingavägen 17a, Saltsjöbaden ▪ 08 717 15 60 ▪ Open Sep–Apr: 10:30am–2pm Mon–Fri; May–Aug: 10:30am–late daily ▪ (Kr)(Kr)

A true archipelago dining experience just a short train from Slussen. Open for lunch all-year round.

⑩ Rökeriet, Fjärderholmarna
Fjärderholmarna ▪ 08 716 50 88 ▪ Open May–early Sep: noon–10pm daily ▪ (Kr)

An idyllic archipelago restaurant, Rökeriet specializes in seafood.

The waterside Rökeriet

Streetsmart

**Pedestrian tunnel in Stockholm's
underground system**

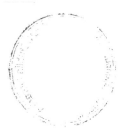

Getting To and Around Stockholm

Arriving by Air

Arlanda Airport is the major international airport in the region, set 37 km (23 miles) north of Stockholm. Direct flights to European and North American destinations are served by carriers including **British Airways**, **KLM**, **Lufthansa**, **Norwegian Air**, **SAS** and other major airlines. Terminals 2 and 5 serve all international flights; domestic flights depart from terminals 3 and 4. The **Arlanda Express** airport train will whisk you to the city centre in 20 minutes. Alternatively you can take a cheaper SL commuter train from the station at Sky City, which takes around 40 minutes into the city centre. The airport coach services also take around 40 minutes. Taxis will go to any city centre destination for a fixed fee.

Stockholm Skavsta Airport, or Nyköping Airport, some 100 km (62 miles) south of Stockholm, is Sweden's main airport for low-cost, no-frills carriers. It caters to flights from several European destinations. Access to Stockholm is via a coach service that takes 80–90 minutes. Alternatively, take a train from nearby Nyköping.

Arriving by Train

Stockholm Central Station is the main rail hub for both intercity and local rail services. There is also a daily express service, which runs every two hours to and from Copenhagen in Denmark via Malmö in Sweden.

The state-owned **Statens Järnvägar** (SJ) runs most of the intercity routes, though there are some private train operators. The lowest fares can be purchased 90 days in advance. Suburban commuter trains are run by the city's local transport authority, **Storstockholms Lokaltrafik** (SL). SL travel cards and tickets are valid on these services.

Arriving by Road

The Öresund toll bridge connects Denmark and Sweden. From there follow the E4, a 550-km (340-mile) continuous motorway to Stockholm. A congestion tax is levied on vehicles within central Stockholm, and parking can be expensive.

Arriving By Boat

There are ferries from Finland (Helsinki and Turku), Estonia (Tallinn) and Latvia (Riga) to Stockholm, operated by two companies, **Tallink Silja Line** – whose ships dock at Värtahamnen in the north east of the city – and **Viking Line**, whose ships dock at Stadsgården, right at the northern edge of Södermalm.

Getting Around by Metro

The regular and efficient underground, *tunnelbana* (or T-bana), is the fastest way to get around town. There are three lines – red, green and blue. Trains run until around midnight on weekdays, and all night on Fridays, Saturdays and the eve of most public holidays.

As with all modes of local transport operated by SL, including buses, trams and the Djurgården ferry, nearly all tickets for the metro can be loaded on to an SL Access card – an electronic smart card. You need to pay a fee for the card itself, but you can reuse your card on future visits. There are also single-use travel cards valid for 75 minutes, and 24 or 72 hours.

Tickets and travel cards are sold at Pressbyrån convenience stores (found at many stations), at the SL Center at T-Centralen metro station and at metro and commuter railway stations. There are also ticket machines at most metro and commuter railway stations.

Getting Around by Bus and Tram

The city has an extensive bus network with some very scenic routes. While most services operate until around midnight, some major routes run all night. There are night bus services seven days a week to many destinations further afield. Be aware that you can't pay for your journey on the bus – you need to have purchased your travel card in advance, or have pre-paid via the SL app or by text message.

The tram network, largely dismantled in 1967, has made a comeback. Preserved as a heritage route, line 7N, between the centre and Waldemarsudde, has been reopened to regular traffic. There is still a vintage tram that runs from spring to autumn.

Getting Around by Local Train

Local trains are cheap and handy for several destinations further afield. The *pendeltåg* (commuter train) network extends from Nynäshamn, 60 km (37 miles) south of the city, to Märsta, near Arlanda Airport, and to the nearby city of Uppsala. The Saltsjöbadan suburban rail provides an easy connection between the city and Saltsjöbaden, while the narrow-gauge Roslagsbanan network serves 39 destinations northeast of Stockholm.

Getting Around by Boat

Boats are mostly run by **Waxholmsbolaget**, providing a vital link to several of the islands in the archipelago, as well as sights in Lake Mälaren. Services in summer are more frequent. You can travel to Djurgården on a ferry from Slussen in just 10 minutes (an SL pass is valid).

Getting Around by Taxi

Taxi Stockholm, **Taxi 020** and **Taxi Kurir** are some reputable companies, and their vehicles are never far away in the city centre. However, these taxis are expensive – a trip from a suburb to the city centre may cost around 300 kr; a short hop across town will rarely be under 150 kr.

Getting Around by Car

Driving in the centre is not encouraged, and parking is expensive and difficult to find. There are 25 park-and-ride stops on the way to central Stockholm to encourage the usage of public transport. Sweden has very tough laws on drinking and driving.

On Foot

Walking is a great way to explore Stockholm. The city has wide pavements, and walking distances between many *tunnelbana* stations are relatively short. Vehicles are always obliged to stop at road crossings. Pathways along quaysides, in parks and along esplanades are usually also shared with cyclists; be sure to stay on the pedestrian side.

By Bicycle

Although it is easy to pedal in the city through its network of bike lanes, the conditions can be difficult in winter. Hire bikes for three days or for the season with **City Bikes** from April to October.

DIRECTORY

ARRIVING BY AIR

Arlanda Airport
w arlanda.se/en

Arlanda Express
w arlandaexpress.com

British Airways
w britishairways.com

KLM
w klm.com

Lufthansa
w lufthansa.com

Norwegian Air
w norwegian.com

SAS
w sas.se/en

Stockholm Skavsta Airport
w skavsta.se/en

ARRIVING BY TRAIN

Statens Järnväg
w sj.se

Storstockholms Lokaltrafik
w sl.se

Stockholm Central Station
w dinstation.se/stockholms-centralstation

ARRIVING BY BOAT

Tallink Silja Line
w tallinksilja.com

Viking Line
w vikingline.se

GETTING AROUND BY BOAT

Waxholmsbolaget
w waxholmsbolaget.se

GETTING AROUND BY TAXI

Taxi 020
w taxi020.se

Taxi Kurir
w taxikurir.se

Taxi Stockholm
w taxistockholm.se

GETTING AROUND BY BICYCLE

City Bikes
w citybikes.se

Practical Information

Passports and Visas

Visitors from outside the European Economic Area (EEA), European Union (EU) and Switzerland need a valid passport to travel to Sweden, as do UK visitors; most other EU nationals need only a valid identity card. Citizens of the USA, Canada and Australia can enter and stay visa-free for 90 days; a Schengen visa will be needed for longer stays (obtain this in advance). Citizens of other countries should check their visa requirements with their local Swedish embassy. The **Swedish Migration Agency** and **Visit Sweden** websites have details.

Customs and Immigration

There are no restrictions for EU citizens if goods are for personal use. Arrivals from outside the EU can import a litre of spirits, four litres of wine or 16 litres of beer, plus 200 cigarettes, 50 cigars, or 250 g of tobacco.

Travel Safety Advice

Visitors can get up-to-date travel safety information from the **UK Foreign & Commonwealth Office**, the **US Department of State** and the **Australian Department of Foreign Affairs and Trade**.

Emergency Numbers

There is one **emergency number** for all services; it will work regardless of whether or not you have international roaming or phone credit. All operators speak English, and interpretation services are also available. You can also contact the police in a **non-emergency**. Crimes such as theft should be reported for insurance purposes – you will then be provided with the necessary documentation. The Swedish police are friendly and helpful, and most of them speak English.

Health

There are no necessary or recommended vaccinations for visiting Sweden, and there are few health hazards in Stockholm. Those who hike, camp or undertake outdoor activities in wooded regions or city parks should take measures to prevent tick bites – a risk of **tick-borne encephalitis** is present throughout the countryside including the Stockholm archipelago. Tap water is drinkable.

Swedish hospitals are excellent. A European Health Insurance Card is needed if you are from the EU/EEA, or else you have to pay the fees yourself. Visitors from other countries should make sure they have some form of health insurance. If you have a European Health Insurance Card when visiting a doctor, you pay the same fee as locals – around 180 kr per visit. A list of doctors is available on the **Healthcare Guide 1177** website. If you need a dentist, **City Dental**, in the city centre, is open all week, and most staff speak English. Fees are payable.

Regulations governing the sales of pharmaceuticals in Sweden are strict; a prescription is often required to purchase medicines that can be bought over the counter in many other countries.

Personal Security

Stockholm is generally a very safe city, and no unusual precautions are necessary except common sense. Pickpockets are the greatest hazard; always keep your valuables safe, since fairly brazen attempts at theft in crowded bars are not uncommon. The weekend drinking crowd can get rowdy late at night around Medborgarplatsen and Stureplan, and in metro stations, but is generally harmless if ignored. Busy nightlife areas and the larger metro stations are generally well policed.

With a strong emphasis on sexual equality, women should feel comfortable in Sweden. Unwelcome attention is rare, and is usually from harmless drunks. Apply common-sense precautions late at night. Sweden is considered to be one of the most gay-friendly countries in the world. Homosexuality has been legal since 1944, and the age of consent was equalized in 1972. The Swedish parliament voted to make same-sex marriages legal in 2009 by an overwhelming majority of 261 to 22.

...ency and ...king

...eden's currency is the ...wedish krona (SEK or kr, plural kronor). Sweden is fast on its way to becoming a fully cashless society with only one per cent of payments now made with cash. Credit cards and debit cards are often the only accepted mode of payment, and are used even for small transactions in shops, museums, bars and restaurants. Avoid taking out large amounts of cash in advance of your trip – you may find yourself unable to spend it.

Telephone and Internet

Mobile phone reception is good throughout the city, even on the underground rail system. Etiquette about usage is relaxed; use common sense and you will be fine. To avoid roaming fees if you are visiting from outside the

EU, buy a local operator's pay-as-you-go SIM card and some credit.

Most people's homes in Stockholm have high-speed broadband, so internet cafés have never really caught on here. Free Wi-Fi access is available almost everywhere, including cafés, bars, restaurants and hotels.

TV, Radio and Newspapers

All hotel rooms typically have a TV with a range of channels. The most common are the Swedish SVT1, SVT2, TV3, TV4 and Channel 5, and the international CNN, Sky News, BBC World News and Eurosport. Foreign movies and TV programmes are usually shown in their original language (with Swedish subtitles).

Catch up on the latest news on Sweden all year round with English broadcasts on **Radio Sweden International**. Weekly

half-hour news bulletins are broadcast at 4:30pm on P2 (FM 89.6) every Monday and Thursday.

The main national Swedish newspapers, *Dagens Nyheter*, *Svenska Dagbladet*, *Aftonbladet* and *Expressen*, all have event listings, or you can pick up the *Metro Stockholm* newspaper for free from stands at all underground stations. The free culture newspaper *Nöjesguiden* can be handy for event listings.

The larger Pressbyrån convenience stores, particularly in the city centre, have a very good stock of international newspapers, often the same day's publication. Make your way to the Pressbyrån branch in Stockholm Central Station for the best selection. Prices are not cheap – expect to pay at least 25 kr for a slimmed-down international version. To keep in touch with Swedish news in English try *The Local*.

DIRECTORY

PASSPORTS AND VISAS

Swedish Migration Agency (Migrationsverket)
🔳 migrationsverket.se

Visit Sweden
🔳 visitsweden.com/passport-and-visas

TRAVEL SAFETY ADVICE

Australian Department of Foreign Affairs and Trade
🔳 dfat.gov.au
🔳 smartraveller.gov.au

UK Foreign & Commonwealth Office
🔳 gov.uk/foreign-travel-advice

US Department of State
🔳 travel.state.gov

EMERGENCY SERVICES

Emergency
📞 112

Non-Emergency
📞 114 14

HEALTH

City Dental
🔳 citydental.se

Healthcare Guide 1177
🔳 1177.se

Tick-Borne Encephalitis
🔳 iamat.org/country/sweden/risk/tick-borne-encephalitis

TV, RADIO AND NEWSPAPERS

Aftonbladet
🔳 aftonbladet.se

Dagens Nyheter
🔳 dn.se

Expressen
🔳 expressen.se

The Local
🔳 thelocal.se

Metro Stockholm
🔳 metro.se/stockholm

Nöjesguiden
🔳 ng.se

Radio Sweden International
🔳 sverigesradio.se

Svenska Dagbladet
🔳 svd.se

Opening Hours

Most tourist attractions and major museums are open all day year-round, though be aware that opening hours are often shorter during the winter months, and some outdoor attractions such as Gröna Lund are only open in spring and summer. Major shops are typically open every day of the year, with business hours of somewhere between roughly 8am and 7pm.

Some restaurants and bars only open in the evenings, and will be closed altogether in the early part of the week. Most city centre bars stay open until midnight or 1am. Late-night bars and clubs stay open until 2am or 3am (a handful until 5am).

The two public holidays always liable to upset the norm regarding opening hours are Christmas and Midsummer *(see p61)* – most establishments will be closed on these days. After Christmas and during summer, particularly around Midsummer, it is normal that a few shops, bars and restaurants will be closed for a few days or even a week or two.

Postal Services

The national post office, **PostNord** (formerly Posten), has leased most of its counter operations to private shops – look out for the blue and yellow PostNord symbol outside newsagents or super markets. Stamps are available from Pressbyrån or 7/11 stores. Post is efficient but expensive. Postboxes are yellow for national and international mail; blue for mail for the Stockholm postcode areas (100–199). The last collections are usually at around 5pm to 6pm and 4pm for further afield.

Time Difference

Stockholm is on Central European Time (CET), one hour ahead of Greenwich Mean Time (GMT) and six hours ahead of US Eastern Standard Time. Swedish summer time begins on the last Sunday in March and ends on the last Sunday in October.

Electrical Appliances

Electricity is 220V and the socket is for the standard continental Europe plug (type C and F). Visitors bringing electrical devices from the UK will need a continental adaptor plug. American appliances will need a transformer.

Weather

Stockholm is a city of wild climatic contrasts. The summer can be unusually warm – hot even – with restaurants spilling out on to the streets. Spring and autumn are both quite brief. Wrap up for winter – the temperature can drop as low as −20° C (−4° F) and some years it rarely rises above zero between November and March.

May through August sees Stockholm in full bloom, and the city is never overcrowded – in high summer you may have some areas almost to yourself as the locals head for the countryside. September is great, with blue skies and pretty foliage. December to February is also a delightful time to visit, even if gets dark around mid-afternoon. Some of the most important events are staged during the run-up to Christmas.

Travellers With Specific Needs

Stockholm prides itself on being one of the most accessible capital cities in the world. The metro is adapted for disabled users with access at all stations, and buses "kneel" at stops to help travellers board and disembark. Additionally, around 360 bus stops in the city have been modified by raising the kerb height. All buses have wheelchair ramps. Most major tourist attractions have disabled access and disabled toilets. For more detailed information visit the **De Handikappades Riksförbund (National Disabled Association)**.

Sources of Information

The main tourist office is at Kulturhuset on Sergels torg, a five-minutes walk from Stockholm Central Station. It is well stocked with guides, maps and leaflets. **Sweden.se**, the official site for information about Sweden, is good for travel and tourism advice. It is entirely multilingual, as is the **Visit Stockholm** site. The **Visit Sweden** site *(see p109)* is also a useful resource.

Trips and Tours

The **Strömma** group has well-organised tours on

...s and boats. Boat
...s range from a quick
...-minute cruise through
...e central canals to a
...eturn voyage along Lake
Mälaren to Drottningholm,
and extensive tours of the
Stockholm Archipelago.

Shopping

Stockholm has a wide
variety of shops, from
international high street
chain stores such as H&M
to a multitude of boutique,
designer and second-
hand emporiums, many
of them clustered around
Östermalm and Gamla
Stan, and the SoFo and
Götgatan neighbourhoods
of Södermalm. Stockholm
has several large depart-
ment stores and galleries,
including **MOOD**, **Åhléns
City**, **Nordiska Kompaniet
(NK)**, **Sturegallerian** and
Gallerian. Prices are
roughly on a par with
what you would expect to
pay for equivalent goods
back home, but there are
always bargains to be
found, particularly during
sales – just look out for
big signs saying *rea*.

Where to Eat

Dining out in Stockholm is
generally pricey, but value
for money is high across
the board. The restaurant
scene is big business in
the capital, making it
varied and competitive.
 Most restaurant dining
is informal, and the dress
code is rarely worth
thinking about, except for
at really high-end places,
particularly Stockholm's
multitude of Michelin-
starred establishments.
 Meals typically follow
the standard three-course
format of *förrätt* (starter),
huvudrätt (main course)
and *efterrätt* (dessert),
although small plates
and sharing meals are
becoming increasingly
common. English-lan-
guage menus are widely
available. Tipping at least
10 per cent is common
courtesy for meals. Most
cafés and restaurants are
child-friendly and will
provide chairs and baby-
change facilities.
 The *Dagens lunch* daily
all-inclusive deals are a
good money saver and

can be filling enough to
set you up for the rest of
the day. Stockholm's
many street-food vendors
and kiosks offer inexpen-
sive and satisfying food
at a reasonable price,
although it is best to use
your own judgement as to
whether it looks like the
standards of quality and
hygiene will be satis-
factory or not.

Where to Stay

Hotels in Stockholm do
not come cheap, but the
upside is that standards
are good across the city
and beyond. Thanks to a
reliable public transport
system that runs all night
at weekends, travellers
on a budget can consider
cheaper options outside
the centre, as well as a
hostel or a B&B.
 All major booking sites
cover the city, including
Last Minute, **Tripadvisor**,
Expedia and **Booking.
com**. Private room or
apartment rental is available through **Airbnb, c/o
Stockholm**, **Red Apple
Apartments** and others.

DIRECTORY

POSTAL SERVICES

PostNord
🆆 postnord.se/en

**TRAVELLERS WITH
SPECIAL NEEDS**

De Handikappades
Riksförbund (National
Disabled Association)
🆆 dhr.se

**SOURCES OF
INFORMATION**

Swede.se
🆆 sweden.se

Visit Stockholm
🆆 visitstockholm.com

TRIPS AND TOURS

Strömma
🆆 stromma.se/en

SHOPPING

Åhlens City
🆆 ahlens.se

Gallerian
🆆 gallerian.se

MOOD
🆆 moodstockholm.se

Nordiska Kompaniet
(NK)
🆆 nk.se

Sturegallerian
🆆 sturegallerian.se

WHERE TO STAY

Airbnb
🆆 airbnb.com

Booking.com
🆆 booking.com

c/o Stockholm
🆆 costockholm.com

Expedia
🆆 expedia.com

Last Minute
🆆 lastminute.com

Red Apple Apartments
🆆 redappleapartments.
com

Tripadvisor
🆆 tripadvisor.com

Places to Stay

PRICE CATEGORIES

For a standard double room and taxes per night during the high season. Breakfast is not included unless specified.

 under 1,500 1,500–2,500 Ⓚ Ⓚ Ⓚ over 500

High-End Hotels

Clarion Sign

MAP K3 ■ Östra Järnvägsgatan 35 ■ 08 676 98 00 ■ www.nordic choicehotels.com ■ Ⓚ

This city-centre hotel reflects the Scandinavian spirit with its classic furniture and black-and-white photographs. The Clarion Sign also has a spa, with a gym, sauna and heated outdoor pool, all with fantastic views across Stockholm.

Elite Eden Park

MAP N1 ■ Sturegatan 22 ■ 08 555 627 00 ■ www. elite.se/eng/edenpark ■ Ⓚ

Ideally located between Stureplan's nightlife district and the peaceful Humlegården, this hotel has an English-style gastropub and an Asian restaurant. There are 124 comfortable rooms, a gymnasium and a sauna. Breakfast is included.

First Hotel Reisen

MAP N5 ■ Skeppsbron 12 ■ 08 22 32 60 ■ www. firsthotels.com ■ Ⓚ Ⓚ

With its great waterside setting close to the Royal Palace, the Reisen is a classic hotel with a maritime theme. All of the standard rooms have views of the Old Town, while the superior rooms look out across the waterfront, and luxury rooms have saunas, Jacuzzis and balconies.

Grand Central by Scandic

MAP K2 ■ Kungsgatan 70 ■ 08 512 520 00 ■ www. scandichotels.com ■ Ⓚ Ⓚ

Housed in a 130-year-old building, the classy Grand Central by Scandic is centrally located close to the railway station and the Arlanda Express (see p106). The hotel has a music focus – guests can order in-room concerts, and there are stages throughout the hotel with live music and DJs every night of the week.

Hotel Rival

MAP C5 ■ Mariatorget 3 ■ 08 545 789 00 ■ www. rival.se ■ Ⓚ Ⓚ

The brainchild of ABBA legend Benny Andersson, Hotel Rival is one of the trendiest places to stay in Stockholm. Situated by a leafy square in the lively Södermalm district, the hotel hosts regular DJ events in its stylish bar. The excellent restaurant has a lovely outdoor terrace in the summer.

Ett Hem

MAP C1 ■ Sköldungagatan 2 ■ 08 20 05 90 ■ www. etthem.se ■ Ⓚ Ⓚ Ⓚ

Luxury central living is what is on offer at Ett Hem, a boutique hotel in a 20th-century former townhouse with green gardens. Each of its 12 rooms is individually decorated with classic Scandinavian furniture, antiques and design.

Grand Hotel

MAP N4 ■ Södra Blasieholmshammen 8 ■ 08 679 35 00 ■ www. grandhotel.se ■ Ⓚ Ⓚ Ⓚ

Sweden's top five-star hotel boasts a great location on the Norrmalm waterfront. This hotel also features two restaurants from Michelin-starred chef Mathias Dahlgren along with the Cadier Bar, renowned for its extraordinary cocktails.

Hotel Diplomat

MAP P3 ■ Strandvägen 7c ■ 08 459 68 00 ■ www. diplomathotel.com ■ Ⓚ Ⓚ Ⓚ

A classical hotel in the heart of Östermalm, an exclusive district of Stockholm, the Hotel Diplomat offers lovely views over the water to nearby Djurgården and Skeppsholmen, with vintage tramcars passing by along Strandvägen in the summer. The plush cocktail bar is a trendy spot to relax in at the end of a day's sightseeing.

Lydmar Hotel

MAP D3 ■ Södra Blasieholmshamnen 2 ■ 08 22 31 60 ■ www. lydmar.com ■ Ⓚ Ⓚ Ⓚ

A luxury hotel with a boutique feel, peacefully overlooking the harbour at Blasieholmen. There is a discreet second-floor terrace for sipping cocktails with sea views. Hotel guests have access to the nearby Grand Hotel's spa and fitness suite.

s Hotel

M2 ■ **Norrmalmstorg**
■ 08 614 10 00
www.nobishotel.se
Ⓚ Ⓚ Ⓚ
At this contemporary
luxury hotel the emphasis
is on timeless chic and
optimum function. Set
in the heart of the city, it
features an Italian-style
restaurant and a more
relaxed bistro, plus the
Gold Bar and Lounge.

Radisson Blu Waterfront Hotel
MAP K4 ■ **Nils Ericssons
Plan 4** ■ 08 505 060 00
■ www.radissonblu.com
■ Ⓚ Ⓚ Ⓚ
Close to Stockholm
Central Station, this hotel
is connected to the
3,000-seater Stockholm
Waterfront Congress
Centre, and is popular for
major business functions.
Its rooms offer excellent
views over the city.
Breakfast is included.

Boutique and Unique Hotels

Elite Hotel Marina Tower
Saltsjöqvarns kaj 25
■ 08 555 702 00 ■ www.
elite.se/stockholm/
marina-tower ■ Ⓚ Ⓚ
A waterfront hotel set
in a former 19th-century
mill on the Nacka shore,
Marina Tower can be
reached by commuter ferry
from the city centre. The
leisure facilities include a
Turkish hammam as well
as a swimming pool.

Hotel with Urban Deli
MAP C2 ■ **Sveavägen 44**
■ 08 30 30 50 ■ www.
hotelwith.se ■ Ⓚ Ⓚ
Having forged a strong
reputation in the food
business, Urban Deli have

opened their first hotel,
which is based entirely
underground. None of the
rooms have windows, but
all of them have a state-
of-the-art air purifying
system, powerful sound
and media systems and
high-speed Wi-Fi access.

Mornington Hotel
MAP N1 ■ **Nybrogatan 53**
■ 08 507 330 00 ■ www.
mornington.se ■ Ⓚ Ⓚ
This charming boutique
hotel is located in the heart
of Östermalm. A library
with 4,000 books is one of
the outstanding features
of this hotel. It also has a
patio garden in summer.

NoFo Hotel
MAP D5 ■ **Tjärhovsgatan
11** ■ 08 503 112 00 ■ www.
nofohotel.se ■ Ⓚ Ⓚ
Constructed in 1780, this
beautiful building was
once a brewery, barracks
and hospital. These days
it's home to the chic
NoFo Hotel. Rooms are
individually decorated and
take inspiration from
Scandinavian retro design
and 1920s Paris.

Story Hotel
MAP N2 ■ **Riddargatan 6**
■ 08 545 039 40 ■ www.
storyhotels.com ■ Ⓚ Ⓚ
A quirky boutique hotel, the
Story is a lively place with
a touch of class. It has a
"retro" modern restaurant,
and DJs play music in the
bar four nights a week.
The hotel offers a variety
of room types from which
to choose.

Villa Källhagen
MAP F3
■ **Djurgårdsbrunnsvägen
10** ■ 08 665 03 00 ■ www.
kallhagen.se ■ Ⓚ Ⓚ
Located by the canal in
Djurgården, this refined

hotel is a peaceful
place to stay and is
within easy reach of
the city centre on public
transport. The rooms
are all tastefully deco-
rated, and the premises
also house a highly
rated restaurant.

The Winery Hotel
Rosenborgsgatan 20
■ 08 14 60 00 ■ www.
the wineryhotel.se
■ Ⓚ Ⓚ
An industrial-chic wine-
themed hotel on the
fringes of Stockholm near
the shores of Brunnsviken
lake, this hotel is within
easy reach of the centre.
There is a restaurant,
wine bar, on-site winery,
gym, and rooftop terrace
with an outdoor pool.

Berns Hotel
MAP M3
■ **Näckströmsgatan 8**
■ 08 566 32 00 ■ www.
berns.se ■ Ⓚ Ⓚ Ⓚ
A boutique hotel, Berns
is right in the city centre
and an ideal choice
for those interested in
the city's nightlife. The
hotel's own nightclub
features world-famous
and top local DJs.

Haymarket by Scandic
MAP C3 ■ **Hötorget
13–15** ■ 08 517 267 00
■ www.scandichotels.
com/haymarket
■ Ⓚ Ⓚ Ⓚ
Inhabiting the former
premises of the famous
old PUB department
store, this indulgent
Scandic signature hotel
harks back to a 1920s
era of optimism and
elegance, with free room
service, a lifestyle
concierge and even
in-room bartenders.

Hotel Skeppsholmen
MAP Q5 ■ Gröna gången 1 ■ 08 407 23 50 ■ www.hotelskeppsholmen.com ■ (Kr)(Kr)(Kr)
This hotel has earned rave reviews as one of the hippest places to stay in the city. It combines the atmosphere of a building from 1699 with modern design and is on a beautiful city island with good bus connections to the centre.

Miss Clara by Nobis
MAP C2 ■ Sveavägen 48 ■ 08 440 67 00 ■ www.missclarahotel.com ■ (Kr)(Kr)(Kr)
This sleek, urban hotel, situated in a former girls' school, is perfectly located for exploring central Stockholm. Expect rooms with cool, modern, black-and-white furnishings, wood parquet floors and designer linens and toiletries. There is a bar and restaurant, too.

Mid-Range Hotels

August Strindberg Hotell
MAP J1 ■ Tegnérgatan 38 ■ 08 32 50 06 ■ www.hotellstrindberg.se ■ (Kr)(Kr)
A lovely little garden where guests enjoy breakfast in summer is the highlight of the August Strindberg. The hotel is tucked away on a quiet side street just off the most interesting part of Drottninggatan and is close to all shops.

Central Hotel
MAP K2 ■ Vasagatan 38 ■ 08 566 208 00 ■ www.central.hotelistockholm.com ■ (Kr)(Kr)
In an excellent location almost opposite the main railway station and ideal for arrivals from all city

airports, the comfortable Central Hotel is renowned for its friendly welcome. It is an affordable option in the heart of the city.

Clarion Hotel Stockholm
MAP D6 ■ Ringvägen 98 ■ 08 462 10 00 ■ www.nordicchoicehotels.com ■ (Kr)(Kr)
The hotel is located in a residential area of Södermalm and is close to the Skanstull Tunnelbana station as well as famous sights such as the Royal Palace and Globen. The cool upstairs bar is a popular meeting spot.

Elite Adlon
MAP K2 ■ Vasagatan 42 ■ 08 402 65 00 ■ www.adlon.se ■ (Kr)(Kr)
With an exterior that evokes the style of the 1950s, this hotel offers all modern facilities. In a busy location close to the city shops, it is also handy for the coach arrivals from the airports.

Elite Hotel Arcadia
MAP D1 ■ Körsbärsvägen 1 ■ 08 566 215 00 ■ www.elite.se ■ (Kr)(Kr)
This hotel is located in a quiet residential area, but the Tekniska Högskolan Tunnelbana station provides quick links to the centre. The Arcadia is also a short stroll to the bars and restaurants of Vasastan. Apartments with kitchenettes cater for guests on longer stays.

Hotel At Six
MAP M3 ■ Brunkebergstorg 6 ■ 08 578 828 00 ■ www.hotelatsix.com ■ (Kr)(Kr)
Centrally located, At Six has over 300 luxurious rooms decorated with

sleek, contemporary furnishings. The hotel's sophisticated restaurant and two stylish bars are popular with the city's residents as well guests. The hotel is also home to Stockholm's only Listening Lounge, an interesting music bar with international DJs, album sessions and lectures.

Hotel Wellington
MAP E2 ■ Storgatan 6 ■ 08 667 09 10 ■ www.wellington.se ■ (Kr)(Kr)
This laid-back and simple Östermalm hotel is well-suited for Skansen and Gröna Lund, along with the Strandvägen waterfront, the tram line and all city centre attractions and amenities. The rooms are very comfortable and individually styled with hardwood floors. Some rooms have balconies. The rate includes breakfast, and there is a sauna and a restaurant.

Park Inn by Radisson Hammarby Sjöstad Hotel
Midskeppsgatan 6 ■ 08 505 070 00 ■ www.parkinn.com ■ (Kr)(Kr)
This hotel offers modern conveniences in one of Stockholm's ecofriendly districts, Hammarby Sjöstad. Its facilities include a sauna, a gym and a restaurant. Skip across the canal by boat, then take a bus to the city centre.

Rex Hotel
MAP C2 ■ Luntmakargatan 73 ■ 08 16 00 40 ■ www.rexhotel.se ■ (Kr)(Kr)
A homely and friendly hotel in a refurbished townhouse dating from 1866, this has exposed

...rick walls and colourful furnishings. Only a block away from Sveavägen, it is in an area with a host of restaurants and bars.

Scandic Anglais

MAP M1 ▪ Humlegårds-gatan 23 ▪ 08 517 340 00 ▪ www.scandichotels.se ▪ (Kr)(Kr)

The buzz in this hotel is all about the music – with DJs playing six nights a week. There are 230 standard rooms with wooden flooring. Dine in its restaurant or pick up a drink from one of its popular bars. A buffet breakfast is included in the rate.

Scandic Continental

MAP C3 ▪ Vasagatan 22 ▪ 08 517 342 00 ▪ www.scandichotels.com ▪ (Kr)(Kr)

Rebuilt to accommodate the construction of a railway tunnel under the site, the Scandic Continental is one of the group's most state-of-the-art hotels. Facilities include a gym, a car park, a good restaurant and several bars, including a lovely rooftop terrace in summer.

Scandic Malmen

MAP D5 ▪ Götgatan 49–51 ▪ 08 517 347 00 ▪ www.scandichotels.com ▪ (Kr)(Kr)

An ideal base for exploring the buzzing heart of the vibrant Södermalm area, the Malmen overlooks large Medborgarplatsen, with SoFo just a couple of minutes' walk away. The hotel features a busy late-night bar-restaurant, while the adjoining Lilla Hotellbaren hosts live DJs and gigs, many of which are free to enter.

Out-of-Town Accommodation

Clarion Hotel Gillet

Dragarbrunnsgatan 23, Uppsala ▪ 01 868 18 00 ▪ www.clarionhotelgillet.com ▪ (Kr)

The location in central Uppsala makes this hotel a good base to explore the city. Clarion Hotel Gillet has modern rooms and music nights in the bar.

Good Morning+ Hagersten

Vastertorpsvägen 131 ▪ 08 556 323 30 ▪ www.ligula.se/goodmorninghotels/hagersten ▪ (Kr)

Located on the southern approach to Stockholm, near the furniture retailer IKEA, this hotel offers high standards at reasonable prices. Its friendly, multilingual staff make it a popular choice.

Jumbo Stay

Jumbovägen 4, Arlanda Airport ▪ 08 593 604 00 ▪ www.jumbostay.com ▪ (Kr)

Anyone who has ever wished to spend a night in their own private bedroom on an aeroplane, can have just that on this converted 747 airliner at Arlanda Airport. It is truly a unique experience.

Kastellet Bed & Breakfast

Vaxholms Kastell, Vaxholm ▪ 08 541 330 35 ▪ www.kastelletbnb.se ▪ (Kr)

Set in the ancient fort of Vaxholm, this B&B is a good base for exploring the archipelago. Most ferries out of central Stockholm stop at this town, and from there it is easy to reach some of the islands by boat in a short time.

Grand Hotel Saltsjöbaden

Hotellvägen 1, Saltsjöbaden ▪ 08 506 170 00 ▪ www.grandsaltsjobaden.se ▪ (Kr)(Kr)

Inspired by the glitzy Hôtel de Paris in Monte-Carlo, this is a majestic hotel. Sitting by an archipelago harbour, it is just 25 minutes by train to Slussen. The hotel often offers some good-value deals.

Grinda Wärdshus

Grinda (archipelago) ▪ 08 542 494 91 ▪ www.grinda.se ▪ (Kr)(Kr)

An old farmhouse set among fields and with an atmospheric summer harbour café-bar, this hotel allows guests to make the most of Grinda island's simple charm. Breakfast is included.

Hotel J

Ellensviksvägen 1, Nacka Strand ▪ 08 601 30 00 ▪ www.hotelj.com ▪ (Kr)(Kr)

By the waterside in the inner archipelago with connections to the city by boat, Hotel J has a New England nautical theme (think wicker and blue and white). It is a great summer destination in which to unwind.

Sigtuna Stads Hotell

Stora Nygatan 3, Sigtuna ▪ 08 592 501 00 ▪ www.sigtunastadshotell.se ▪ (Kr)(Kr)

This is Sweden's smallest five-star hotel. Dating from 1909, Sigtuna Stads has been very tastefully restored to retain its original elegance. During the summer guests can eat dinner overlooking the picturesque waters of Sigtunaviken.

For a key to hotel price categories see p112

Stallmästaregården Hotel

Norrtull ■ 08 610 13 00 ■ www.stallmastare garden.se ■ (Kr)(Kr)
A former coaching inn from the 1700s, this hotel, set close to Hagaparken, overlooks Brunnsviken lake. Although further afield, it is still a reasonable walk or a short bus ride to bars and restaurants around Odenplan.

Yasuragi Hasseludden

Hamndalsvägen 6, Saltsjö-Boo ■ 08 747 64 00 ■ www.yasuragi.se ■ (Kr)(Kr)
This unusual spa hotel offers both western and traditional Japanese rooms as well as a variety of rejuvenating treatments (including a complimentary dinner). There is also a tranquil Japanese-style garden leading down to the water.

Budget Hotels

Connect Hotel City

MAP A2 ■ Alströmergatan 41 ■ 08 441 02 20 ■ www. connecthotel.se ■ (Kr)
Quite basic in its approach, with some very small rooms, this hotel offers good rates for its location in the liveliest part of Kungsholmen. Try to make the most of the early booking discount.

Hotel Attaché

Cedergrensvägen 16, Hägersten ■ 08 18 11 85 ■ www.aparthotel.se ■ (Kr)
A little out of town in a quiet residential area, Attaché has 60 rooms in varying sizes to choose from, and breakfast is included in the room prices. The hip Landet bar

and restaurant is nearby if you want to go out in the neighbourhood.

Hotel Bema

MAP C2 ■ Upplandsgatan 13 ■ 08 23 26 75 ■ www. hotelbema.se ■ (Kr)
Facing the Tegnérlunden park and with an indoor courtyard garden, Bema has a pleasant location, right in the city. It is a good choice for anyone looking for a central hotel at a fair price.

Hotel Micro

MAP C2 ■ Tegnérlunden 8 ■ 08 545 455 69 ■ www. hotelmicro.se ■ (Kr)
The theme of this hotel is small rooms at small prices. The rooms are windowless and bathroom facilities shared, but if the aim is to explore the city and you want a central place to sleep, it offers a genuine budget price.

Hotel Tre Små Rum

MAP C5 ■ Högbergsgatan 81 ■ 08 641 23 71 ■ www. tresmarum.se ■ (Kr)
This is a superb-value option in a convenient location in Södermalm, close to the Tunnelbana and local train stations. The rooms are cozy and comfortable; breakfast is included in the price.

Motel L Hammarby Sjöstad

Hammarby allé 41 ■ 08 409 026 00 ■ ligula.se/ motel-l ■ (Kr)
Modern design comes at a budget price at Motel L, where all rooms have Swedish Carpe Diem beds, rain showers and air conditioning. The communal area is a big, bright space where guests can rest, work or have a drink.

Quality Hotel Nacka

Värmdövägen 84, Nacka ■ 08 506 160 00 ■ www. choicehotels.se ■ (Kr)
Alongside a pool, sauna and a decent restaurant, this has 162 comfortable rooms. In summer, guests can enjoy a meal or drink on the beautiful terrace. There is free parking outside the entrance.

The Red Boat Hotel

MAP C4 ■ Söder Mälarstrand Kajplats 10 ■ 08 644 43 85 ■ www. theredboat.com ■ (Kr)
A novel place to stay is on this boat moored close to the Old Town. There are actually two boats – a hotel and a hostel; the wooden-panelled cabins on the hotel boat are the coziest option.

Unique Hotel

MAP K1 ■ Kammakargatan 62 ■ 08 796 96 00 ■ www. uniquehotel.se ■ (Kr)
Located very close to the bustling shopping street Drottninggatan, the Unique Hotel offers large rooms with high ceilings and mullioned windows. Choose between a room with a private bathroom or shared facilities.

Hotel Anno 1647

MAP D5 ■ Mariagränd 3 ■ 08 442 16 80 ■ www. anno1647.se ■ (Kr)(Kr)
Situated in two former townhouses from the 17th and 18th centuries, Anno 1647 is on a side street just off Götgatan, one of Södermalm's main shopping and drinking streets. The hotel is just a few steps away from the Slussen Tunnelbana and bus station, making for excellent transport links.

Hotel Zinkensdamm

MAP B5 ▪ Zinkens Väg 20 ▪ 08 616 81 10 ▪ www.zinkensdamm.com ▪ ⓚⓚ

Situated in Tantolunden park on Södermalm, Hotel Zinkensdamm includes breakfast and internet access in its price; it has a bar and restaurant, too. It is both a hotel and hostel, and is a pleasant place to stay. There are bicycles available for hire.

B&Bs, Hostels and Apartments

Bed & Breakfast Stockholm at Mariatorget

MAP C5 ▪ Torkel Knutssonsgatan 35 ▪ 07 057 972 00 ▪ www.bedbreakfaststockholm.com ▪ ⓚ

Set in the same building as the entrance to the Mariatorget Tunnelbana station are these modern rooms. There are two one- or two-person rooms available, or both can be booked to accommodate three or four people as there is a connecting door.

Biz Apartment Gärdet

Sehlstedtsgatan 4 ▪ 08 578 553 00 ▪ www.bizapartmenthotel.se/gardet ▪ ⓚ

This hotel has 175 classy apartments; choose between one- and two-bedroom apartments or a range of studios that are ideal for the solo traveller. There are some good deals for those wanting extended stays of a few weeks or months. Biz also has other hotels at Solna and Hammarby Sjöstad.

City Backpackers Inn

MAP K2 ▪ Upplandsgatan 2a ▪ 08 20 69 20 ▪ www.citybackpackers.org ▪ ⓚ

This classic hostel has plenty of character, free internet, free pasta, laundry, a guest kitchen and very helpful staff. There is a variety of rooms from which to choose.

Globen Bed & Breakfast

Dammtrappgatan 13 ▪ 07 367 980 60 ▪ www.globenvilla.se ▪ ⓚ

Live like a local in a typical Swedish wooden house with a pretty garden in a residential part of Stockholm near Globen and its underground station. There is a fully equipped cottage and also a studio.

Hostel af Chapman

MAP P5 ▪ Flaggmansvägen 8 ▪ 08 463 22 66 ▪ www.svenskaturistforeningen.se ▪ ⓚ

Stay on a 19th-century ship on Skeppsholmen, overlooking the Royal Palace and near many of the city's main museums. For the best value, take a bed in a shared cabin, though there are private rooms available, too.

Långholmen Hotel and Youth Hostel

MAP A5 ▪ Långholmsmuren 20 ▪ 08 720 85 00 ▪ www.langholmen.com ▪ ⓚ

Staying in a prison cell may not be everyone's dream – but that is the unique appeal of this former jail, which saw its last prisoners in 1975. It is now a fantastic modern hotel and hostel on the central island of Långholmen.

Lunda Pensionat

MAP B5 ▪ Lundagatan 31 ▪ 07 364 357 69 ▪ www.lundapensionat.se ▪ ⓚ

On a pleasant street close to the Zinkensdamm Tunnelbana station, this has double rooms with views over Lake Mälaren and the city. It also has ship-cabin-style rooms. Guests can make use of the fully equipped kitchen.

Stockholm Hostel

MAP A2 ▪ Alströmergatan 15 ▪ 07 015 655 25 ▪ www.stockholmhostel.se ▪ ⓚ

This air-conditioned hostel is in Kungsholmen, a five-minute ride on the Tunnelbana from Stockholm Central station. Each room has a private bathroom. Guests can prepare meals in the two communal kitchens.

Guldgränd Hotel Apartments

MAP D5 ▪ Guldgränd 5 ▪ 08 641 40 64 ▪ www.secondhomeapartments.se/guldgränd ▪ ⓚⓚ

In a 17th-century building not far from the Slussen Tunnelbana station in a busy part of Södermalm, Guldgränd has spacious and stylish single, double and triple rooms as well as family apartments.

Rygerfjord Hotel and Hostel

MAP C4 ▪ Söder Mälarstrand, Kajplats 12–14 ▪ 08 84 08 30 ▪ www.rygerfjord.se ▪ ⓚⓚ

A former Norwegian ferry boat, this has been converted into a hotel and hostel while retaining its nautical feel. Some rooms overlook Lake Mälaren with fine views across to the City Hall.

For a key to hotel price categories see p112

Index

Acknowledgments

Author

Paul Eade was born and raised in Scarborough, England, but has lived in Stockholm since 1999. He enjoys travelling, particularly in Germany.

Additional contributor
Malcolm Jack

Publishing Director Georgina Dee

Publisher Vivien Antwi

Design Director Phil Ormerod

Editorial Sophie Adam, Ankita Awasthi Tröger, Rachel Fox, Maresa Manara, Freddie Marriage, Sally Schafer, Hollie Teague

Cover Design Richard Czapnik

Design Marisa Renzullo, Bhavika Mathur

Commissioned Photography James Tye, Jeppe Wikstrom

Picture Research Susie Peachey, Ellen Root, Lucy Sienkowska

Cartography Subhashree Bharati, Mohammad Hassan, James Macdonald, Casper Morris

DTP Jason Little

Production Igrain Roberts

Factchecker Taraneh Ghajar Jerven

Proofreader Clare Peel

Indexer Helen Peters

Picture Credits

The publisher would like to thank the following for their kind permission to reproduce their photographs:
Key: a-above; b-below/bottom; c-centre; f-far; l-left; r-right; t-top

123RF.com: Jon Bilous 64cla; Boris Breytman 30bc; Hans Christiansson 66b; Ievgenii Fesenko 77tr; Veronika Galkina 77b; Stefan Holm 19cl; jorisvo 40cla; Mikhail Markovskiy 76tr; Olga Miltsova 100-1; svglass 39tr.

Alamy Stock Photo: Rolf Adlercreutz 61tl; Banana Pancake 4cr; Frank Chmura 48t, 55bl, 101cl; Mikael Damkier 82-3; Chad Ehlers 58tr, 93b; Peter Forsberg 53b, 94-5; Bjorn Grotting 35crb; Dave G. Houser 31tl; imageBROKER / Matthias Graben 4clb; Johner Images 35bl, 61br; Interfoto 11clb; Art Kowalsky 78-9; Douglas Lander 103b; Franz Marc Frei 18tr; Hercules Milas 11tl; Prisma by Dukas Presseagentur GmbH / Chmura Frank 46tr; Maria Swärd 16-7; William Uzuriaga 60ca; Zoonar / Olaf Pokorny 11br; ZUMA Press, Inc. 52clb.

© ArkDes: Nikolaj Alsterdal 88t.

AWL Images: Mauricio Abreu 12-3; David Bank 4cla; Nordic Photos 2tl, 4cl, 4b, 8-9.

Operaka ällarens Bakficka: 69br.

Bonniers Konsthall: 72cla.

Brewdog Kungsholmen: Mikael Goransson 74b.

Centralbadet, Stockholm: Magnus Torle 67cl.

Designtorget: Jean-Baptiste Beranger 56tr.

Dorling Kindersley: The Golden Hall, Stockholm Stadshuset by Einar Forseth © DACS 2017 22-3.

Dreamstime.com: Arsty 84tr; Ruzanna Arutyunyan 10cla; Roksana Bashyrova 85t; Per Björkdahl 17br, 99tr; Andrei Bortnikau 40bl; Boris Breytman 6cla, 25tl; Ryhor Bruyeu 41tr; Candy1812 10cl; Hans Christiansson 34clb; Marcin Ciesielski / Sylwia Cisek 22br, 23cr; Cumulus 72-3; Mikael Damkier 23tl; Dimbar76 57tr; Eugenephoen 2tr, 36-7; Alexandre Fagundes De Fagundes 58-9; Kaleff 10cb, 11cra, 24-5, 42-3, 44b; Sergii Koval 55tr; Andrey Kutsenko 23br; Alain Lacroix 4crb; Mariagroth 59tr, 71b, 73tl; Mikhail Markovskiy 30-1, 86cl, 86br; Julie Mayfeng 49br; Moniphoto 100tr; Nadezhda 1906 59br; Nikonaft 87tl; Pifu 70ca; Theresa Wing Yee Poon 6br; Rolf52 45tl, 60b; André Sandberg 7tr; Tatiana Savvateeva 98ca; Scanrail 28-9; Tatjanagrzan 47tl; Tibisan 17cr; Allan Wallberg 19tr.

Earth N More: 89cl.

© Fotografiska, Jenny Hammar: 94cl.

Gastrologik: Erik Olsson Photography 54cb.

Getty Images: Mauricio Abreu 78tl; Bettmann 39l; DEA / A. Dagli Orti 38ca; Elliot Elliot 19b; Werner Forman 100c; Johner Images 18bl; Ullstein Bild 38bl.

Grand Hôtel Stockholm: The Cadier Bar / Magnus Mårding 90b; Mathias Dahlgren / Magnus Mårding 54t.

Grandpa: 57cl.

Greasy Spoon: 53tr.

Grill: 75cra.

Gröna Lund: 28bl, 29bl, 49cl; Frans Hällquist 29cr.

Hornstulls Marknad: Patrik Linden Photography 46br.

Hotel Skeppsholmen: Restaurant La ånga Raden / Louise Billgert 91cra.

iStockphoto.com: adisa 1; cosmity 10b; fotoVoyager 3tl, 4t, 62-3; master1305 11crb; olaser 3tr, 104-5.

Junibacken: 48clb.

Kulturhuset: Matilda Rahm 65b.

Kungliga Operan: Markus Gårder 65tl.

Restaurang Kvarnen: Ivan da SIlva 50-1, 96tr.

Marie Laveau Club: 51tr.

Moderna Museet: Åsa Lundén 43tl.

Naturhistoriska riksmuseet: Martin Stenmark 99br.

Restaurant Pelikan: Christer Fahlström 97br.

Riche: Niklas Alexandersson 80cl.

The Royal Court (Kungliga Hovstaterna): 27tl; Alexis Daflos 20-1, 24br, 25br, 26cl, 26bc, 26-7, 85br; Gomer Swahn 35cra.

Skansen: Marie Andersson 13cr; Marie Ha åkansson 12bl; Bo Jonsson 13tl.

Sofo: Justina Rosengren 92tl.

Spiritmuseum: Jonas Lindstro öm 47cr.

Statens Hstoriska Museum: 33tl; Magnus Aronson 33c; Gabriel Hildebrand 32br; Katarina Nimmervoll 32ca, 33crb.

SuperStock: age fotostock / Jörgen Larsson 45cr; Fine Art Images 43cr; Nordic Photos 16bl, 34-5, 50cra.

© **SvenHarrys Konstmuseum:** Per Myrehed 71tr.

Sveskt Tenn: 56b.

Tom Tits Experiment: 102tr.

Tyresta National Park: Charl Mellin 102clb.

Världskulturmuseerna Stockholm: Ove Kaneberg 66tl.

Vasamuseet: Anneli Karlsson 14cl, 15br; Karolina Kristensson 15tl.

Vete-Katten: Susanna Bla åvarg 68t.

Cover

Front and spine: **500px:** Domingo Leiva

Back: **Dreamstime.com:** Mikael Damkier

Pull Out Map Cover

500px: Domingo Leiva

All other images © Dorling Kindersley
For further information see:
www.dkimages.com

Penguin
Random
House

Printed and bound in China

First published in Great Britain in 2018
by Dorling Kindersley Limited
80 Strand, London WC2R 0RL

Copyright 2013, 2018 © Dorling
Kindersley Limited

A Penguin Random House Company

18 19 20 21 10 9 8 7 6 5 4 3 2 1

Reprinted with revisions 2013, 2015, 2018

A CIP catalogue record is available from the British Library.

ISBN 978 0 2413 1029 8

MIX
Paper from
responsible sources
FSC™ C018179

SPECIAL EDITIONS OF DK TRAVEL GUIDES

DK Travel Guides can be purchased in bulk quantities at discounted prices for use in promotions or as premiums. We are also able to offer special editions and personalized jackets, corporate imprints, and excerpts from all of our books, tailored specifically to meet your own needs.

To find out more, please contact:

in the US
specialsales@dk.com

in the UK
travelguides@uk.dk.com

in Canada
specialmarkets@dk.com

in Australia
penguincorporatesales@ penguinrandomhouse.com.au

As a guide to abbreviations in visitor information blocks: **Adm** = *admission charge*

Phrase Book

When reading the imitated pronunciation, stress the part which is underlined. Pronounce each syllable as if it formed part of an English word, and you will be understood sufficiently well. Remember the points below, and your pronunciation will be even closer to the correct Swedish.

Guidelines for Pronunciation

ai = as in 'fair' or 'stair'
ea = as in 'ear' or 'hear'
ew = like the sound in 'dew'
EW = try to say 'ee' with your lips rounded
oo = as in 'book' or 'soot'
OO = as in 'spoon' or 'groom'
r = should be strongly pronounced

Swedish Alphabetical Order

In the list below we have followed the Swedish alphabetical order. The following letters are listed after z: å, ä, ö.

In an Emergency

Help!	Hjälp!	yelp
Stop!	Stanna!	stanna!
Call a doctor!	Ring efter en doktor!	ring efter ehn doktor
Call an ambulance!	Ring efter en ambulans!	ring efter ehn ambewlanss
Call the police!	Ring polisen!	ring poleesen
Call the fire brigade!	Ring efter brandkåren!	ring efter brandkawren
Where is the nearest telephone?	Var finns närmaste telefon?	vahr finnss nairmasteh telefawn
Where is the nearest hospital?	Var finns närmaste sjukhus?	vahr finnss nairmasteh shewkhews

Communication Essentials

Yes	Ja	yah
No	Nej	nay
Please (offering)	Varsågod	vahrshawgOOd
Thank you	Tack	tack
Excuse me	Ursäkta	ewrshekta
Hello	Hej	hay
Goodbye	Hej då/adjö	haydaw/ahyur
Good night	God natt	goonutt
Morning	Morgon	morron
Afternoon	Eftermiddag	eftermiddahg
Evening	Kväll	kvell
Yesterday	Igår	ee gawr
Today	Idag	ee dahg
Tomorrow	I morgon	ee morron
Here	Här	hair
There	Där	dair
What?	Vad?	vah
When?	När?	nair
Why?	Varför?	vahrfurr
Where?	Var?	vahr

Useful Phrases

How are you?	Hur mår du?	hewr mawr dew
Very well, thank you.	Mycket bra, tack.	mewkeh brah, tack
Pleased to meet you.	Trevligt att träffas.	treavlit att traiffas
See you soon.	Vi ses snart.	vee seas snahrt
That's fine.	Det går bra.	dea gawr brah
Where is/are …?	Var finns …?	vahr finnss…
How far is it to …?	Hur långt är det till …?	hewr lawngt er dea till
Which way to …?	Hur kommer jag till …?	hewr kommer yah till …

Do you speak English?	Talar du/ni engelska?	tahlar dew/nee engelska
I don't understand	Jag förstår.	yah furshtawr inteh
Could you speak more slowly, please?	Kan du/ni tala långsammare, tack.	kan dew/nee tahla lawng-ssamareh tack
I'm sorry.	Förlåt.	furrlawt

Useful Words

big	stor	stOOr
small	liten	leeten
hot	varm	varrm
cold	kall	kall
good	bra	brah
bad	dålig	dawleeg
enough	tillräcklig	tillraikleeg
open	öppen	urpen
closed	stängd	staingd
left	vänster	vainster
right	höger	hurger
straight on	rakt fram	rahkt fram
near	nära	naira
far	långt	lawngt
up/over	upp/över	ewp/urver
down/under	ner/under	near/ewnder
early	tidig	teedee
late	sen	sehn
entrance	ingång	ingawng
exit	utgång	ewtgawng
toilet	toalett	too-alett
more	mer	mehr
less	mindre	meendre

Shopping

How much - is this?	Hur mycket - kostar den här?	hewr mewkeh kostar dehn hair
I would like …	Jag skulle vilja…	yah skewleh vilya
Do you have?	Har du/ni …?	hahr dew/nee …
I'm just looking	Jag ser mig bara omkring	yah sear may bahra omkring
Do you take credit cards?	Tar du/ni kreditkort?	tahr dew/nee kredeetkoort
What time do you open?	När öppnar ni?	nair urpnar nee
What time do you close?	När stänger ni?	nair stainger nee
expensive	dyr	dewr
cheap	billig	billig
size (clothes)	storlek	stOOrlek
white	vit	veet
black	svart	svart
red	röd	rurd
yellow	gul	gewl
green	grön	grurn
blue	blå	blaw
antique shop	antikaffär	anteek-affair
bakery	bageri	bahgeree
bank	bank	bank
book shop	bokhandel	bOOkhandel
cake shop	konditori	konditoree
chemist	apotek	apoteak
market	marknad	marrknad
newsagent	tidningskiosk	teednings-cheeosk
post office	postkontor	posstkontOOr
supermarket	snabbköp	snabbchurp
tobacconist's	tobakshandel	tOObaks-handel
travel agency	resebyrå	reasseh-bewraw

Sightseeing

art gallery	konstgalleri	konnst-galleree
church	kyrka	chewrka
garden	trädgård	traidgawrd
house	hus	hews